Behind the Mask

Behind the Mask

Embrace Risk and DARE to Be Better

Donald F. Hastings

Chairman Emeritus

The Lincoln Electric Company

and

Leslie Anne Hastings

Library of Congress Control Number: 2014916187
ISBN: Hardcover   978-1-4990-7127-6
                   Softcover   978-1-4990-7128-3
                   eBook   978-1-4990-7129-0

Rev. date: 11/03/2014

Front cover watercolor of Don Hastings painted by Molly (Boren) Whitney

Back cover photo of Don Hastings compliments of The Lincoln Electric Company, Cleveland, OH, USA.

Back cover photo of Leslie Hastings compliments of Wells Photography, Denver, CO, USA.

Permission to reprint or modify portions of "Harsh Lessons from International Expansion," by Donald F. Hastings (Harvard Business Review #99305) granted by Harvard Business School Publishing

To order additional copies of this book, contact:
Xlibris
1-888-795-4274
www.Xlibris.com
Orders@Xlibris.com
656850

For Shirley,

Best friend, lover, co-conspirator
and trophy wife for sixty years.

"It's kind of fun to do the impossible"

~Walt Disney

Contents

FYI

Arc Welding and the Mask

ARC WELDING IS a type of welding that uses a welding power supply to create an electric arc between an electrode and the base material to melt the metals at the welding point. Today it remains an important process for the fabrication of steel buildings, bridges, vehicles, ships, tanks, construction and farm equipment, power plants, and pipelines. In fact, just about anything manufactured with metal is arc welded.

The Lincoln Electric Company, based in Cleveland, Ohio, is the world's leader in manufacturing and selling arc welding equipment and consumables. Because of the intense ultraviolet light, the 1300-degree heat of the arc and the particulate metal spatter created by the welding process, the welding operator wears a helmet, or "mask," for protection.

Say, who IS that masked man?

PREFACE

A Few Minutes with Don Hastings

This book is not meant to teach but to *inspire*.

There are plenty of books, articles, and business school case studies spotlighting the Lincoln Electric Company and its famous management system, combining profit sharing, pay for performance, and guaranteed employment.

This is not one of them.

Rather, this book is the story of how I used highly unorthodox methods to rise from sales trainee to Chief Executive Officer and Chairman of the Board in one of the most unique manufacturing companies in the world.

It is a story of embracing risk and daring to be better.

I can't teach you how to embrace risk. No one can. I CAN show you what embracing risk looks like and urge you to take chances. When you play it safe, nothing moves. Excitement and progress lie on the edge of the known–for better or for worse.

Throughout my forty-four years at Lincoln, I utilized decidedly unconventional methods to solve problems—not many companies hire nearly *one thousand additional people* during the peak of a financial crisis. My tactics weren't always popular, and in a couple of instances, I'm surprised I didn't get myself fired as I tripped over rigid policies, entrenched philosophies, and stubborn personalities.

That being said, my penchant for turning obstacles into "opportunities to be creative" led Lincoln to manufacture new product lines, avoid downsizing during economic slumps, and create THE MIRACLE ON ST. CLAIR. Unorthodox ideas enabled me not only to rise to the top of the organization but also, as CEO, to lead Lincoln out of the most catastrophic financial situation in its one-hundred-year history and into record sales and profits—without laying off a single US employee.

Not ONE.

If you dare to combine imagination, creativity and innovation with great courage and infinite possibilities, I can't promise you that life will always be a bed of roses, but I can promise you that it will be one *helluva* ride.

FOREWORD

A Modern-Day Camelot

By S. Peter Ullman

THROUGHOUT HIS CAREER, Donald F. Hastings was more than a charismatic, inspirational leader. He had that certain *je ne sais quoi* that all great men seem to possess. This is his story, but it would be incomplete without a few words from one of his "troops" describing the magic of his leadership. I have never met anyone like Don; whatever that "certain something" was, it rubbed off on all of us.

Don hired me as a very green and naive sales trainee fresh out of engineering school at Cornell. Through Don's example and guidance, I found direction, fulfillment, fun, and dedication to a career of advancement at Lincoln Electric that culminated as CEO of Harris Calorific. But beyond me, I watched him inspire the entire sales force and later the entire Lincoln Electric Company to achieve success repeatedly under the most trying of circumstances, all without sacrificing any of the principles that underpinned the Lincoln Electric philosophy. Don was the epitome of charisma, integrity, dedication, and hard work, and under his influence, the entire Lincoln Electric company truly came together as a family. Those years were a magical time in the company's history and one of the primary reasons the company stands strong today.

This book reveals many creative ideas and actions Don conceived to save the day, but it does not adequately explain why thousands of employees performed *beyond their perceived capabilities* to implement them. In my eyes, the answer is rooted in six key leadership traits of Don Hastings:

1. **Encouragement and positive reinforcement are more powerful than criticism and rebuke.** Don was always catching people doing something *right*, with positive reinforcement that inspired them to greater and greater efforts. He always knew of his people's successes, most times without them having to tell him, and he gave them credit for their victories. When someone did let him down, he was brilliant at being able to separate the person from the act. He never openly criticized anyone.

2. **Cultivate personal relationships.** I was privileged to enjoy an extremely close personal relationship with the entire Hastings family. Don's integrity and high personal values had a profound impact on me. I found myself bound to him out of mutual loyalty and respect. I know he touched all "his guys" in the same way, as he invested himself personally in everyone. In return, he was rewarded with loyalty, devotion, and exceptional performance. Don developed this trait as a salesman and refined it to an *art* as a leader.

3. **Love to win, hate to lose, and win without sacrificing personal or company integrity.** Don Hastings was a winner and focused all his energy to that end in every situation. On many occasions, Don was constrained by economic conditions outside his control, by company principles, and by his own personal morality. He could have compromised, but he would not. The true genius behind his creative ideas was that he was able to embrace these constraints and achieve extraordinary success within them. He was a master at maneuvering his way around seemingly impossible situations to produce astounding results.

4. **Never let the troops see you down.** In this book, Don recounts many drastic crises, both personal and professional, that would have wilted most leaders. But we never saw him "down" or heard him complain. He somehow managed to maintain his smile and a positive attitude 24-7. It's nearly impossible for the troops to see this kind of strength and conviction in the face of adversity and not rededicate ourselves to do the same.

5. **Appreciate each employee's special skills, focus on their "positives," and put them in a position to win.** Don always found the best in each person. By using that awareness to define them, he related positively to everyone. He was particularly adept at placing people where their talents yielded success.

6. **Don led from in front, not from behind.** Because Don had come up through the ranks and served his time in the trenches, we knew there was nothing we were facing or would ever face in our jobs that he had not personally experienced. He never expected anything from us that he wouldn't expect from himself. On more than a few occasions, he took undeserved "bullets" for his troops. He never sacrificed one of us for his own glory but continually sacrificed himself for ours.

Don Hastings didn't just practice these concepts—he *lived* them each and every day. To use a military analogy: certainly as ambitious, motivated employees, we wanted to *take that hill* for our bonuses and for our careers; but most of all, we wanted to take that hill for Don Hastings.

Inspired leadership moves mountains.

There are thousands of employees who accomplished the herculean tasks described in the following pages. And in the process, they achieved it with remarkable zeal and a deep sense of personal fulfillment. Therein lies the true *magic* of Donald F. Hastings. His legacy is contained not only in what he did for the Lincoln Electric Company, but perhaps more in what he did for the people—the thousands and thousands of people—that he touched and inspired throughout his life.

People like me.

-1-

Be Careful What You
Ask For

A T 5:01 P.M. on the last Friday of
July 1992, I took over as Chairman
and CEO of the Lincoln Electric Company. I had worked at Lincoln for
thirty-eight years and had reached the pinnacle of my career.

My exhilaration lasted exactly twenty-four minutes.

At 5:25 p.m., while I was engaged in celebratory small talk in the
hallway, our chief financial officer marched up to me and announced,
"I've got some grim news. The numbers just came in from the European
operations- and they're bad. Very bad. They lost almost $7.5 million in
June, and that means we'll have to report a second-quarter loss. We'll
violate our covenants with the banks and default on our loans."

What?

JESUS!

I struggled not to swallow my tongue.

My thoughts immediately raced ahead to December, when we were scheduled to pay out the annual incentive bonus to our US workforce. Despite a soft economy, our operations in the United States had done well. Our three thousand US workers would expect to receive, as a group, more than $50 million. If we were in default, we might not be able to pay them. But if we didn't pay the bonus, the whole company might unravel.

Lincoln Electric's incentive system was created in 1934, and the company has paid significant bonuses every year since. Historically, bonuses have constituted more than 70 percent of our US employees' annual incomes. That system has allowed our people to rank among the highest paid factory workers in the world. Hundreds of them have earned $70,000 to $80,000 in a year, and several handfuls have made more than $100,000.

To someone like me who was raised at Lincoln, not paying the bonus was unimaginable.

That July night was horrible. I couldn't sleep. My thoughts ran back over the day's events. At 4:59 p.m. that Friday, I had been President of Lincoln Electric North America, a healthy company by any standard. From 5:01–5:24 p.m., I had been celebrating my dream job, CEO of a successful and rapidly expanding global organization.

At 5:25p.m., the world crashed down around me. Headlines swam through my head: "New Lincoln CEO Fumbles in First 24 Minutes on the Job." I kept hearing J. F. Lincoln's voice in my head: "OK, Don, you've always wanted the top job. Now it's yours. How are you going to fix this mess?"

That night, I had no answers. In fact, it would be almost two years before I had completely answered that question.

Then I had an idea.

-2-

Beware of False
Gods

IN THE SPRING of 1953, I graduated from Harvard Business School with an MBA in marketing. A Southern California native, I had jumped at the chance to explore the East Coast.

To my surprise, I had fallen in love with New England (especially in the fall) during the two years I'd spent happily ensconced within the hallowed walls of that illustrious institution. Unlike the undergraduate college nestled within the bustling city of Cambridge, the Harvard Business School campus is situated, with picturesque style, on the Boston bank of the Charles River. "The Charles" was often dappled with crew skulls and petite sailing craft and I spent many a brief respite perched atop Weeks Bridge enjoying the maritime parade.

I'll never forget the night I spent whizzing down Boston's Route 9, plastered to the roof of my classmate's 1951 Ford sedan, gripping the top through the cracks in the windows. (No risk was too great to woo the women at Wellesley College!) I have no idea why I didn't drive my own car that night, but I suspect that there may have been more than a little alcohol involved.

Although Boston was magical (and occasionally thrilling), I still had vivid memories of cruising along the Pacific Coast Highway in a shiny new convertible with a beautiful blonde at my side (yes, really). And I planned to have many more. I definitely had to get back to LA.

Blondes and convertibles aside, earlier that year, the Lincoln Electric Company, one of the largest manufacturers of arc welding equipment in the world, had been one of our case studies and (although it was based in Cleveland, Ohio) I was fascinated by the company. Lincoln based its success on a unique set of principles:

- Individual accountability for quality

- Individual responsibility for output

- Compensation (wages and bonuses) tied directly to quality and output

- Maintaining the fewest layers of management possible

That same spring, J. F. Lincoln, one of the founders of the company, gave a talk at the business school. JF was an imposing figure, almost 6'2", with an electric presence. He spoke with passion and immense zeal. I was mesmerized both by the man and by his message.

Lincoln Electric was unique. Here was a company that paid its employees according to their actual contribution to the bottom line. JF spoke of a work environment dedicated to encouraging individual achievement. I liked the sound of that. He spoke of accountability, responsibility, and job security–the very principles that my father had preached to me throughout my childhood. As a son of the Great Depression, I had held a job since the age of nine. I mowed lawns, delivered newspapers and groceries on my bike, and detailed and polished cars. I even worked for several years after school and during the summers for a small firm recovering golf balls (like everything else, new balls were scarce during the war).

During his talk, JF emphasized that top management was committed to setting an example of consistently ethical behavior. My father, a small-business owner in Los Angeles and a complete optimist, had raised me to always take the high road in life. To him, ethics were everything.

As I worked with him evenings in his business, I can remember my dad telling me, "There will be times in your life when you will be faced with different approaches to solving problems. Some may be devious, dishonest, or just not completely straightforward. These choices may benefit you in some way in the short run, either monetarily or otherwise, but they could also tarnish your reputation.

"Your reputation will be the single most important factor to your success and happiness in life. From an ethical standpoint, even if no else knows of even the slightest transgression on your part, YOU will know it. Don't be tempted by anyone you don't trust or with anything you don't feel completely right about."

As JF spoke, he aligned more and more with these principles. I wanted to hear more.

After he finished speaking, he asked the audience if anyone would be interested in speaking to him about a sales position with Lincoln. I immediately signed up. At that time, big corporations were stable entities and manufacturing companies were solid, reliable places within which an individual could achieve unlimited success.

Although I was only thirteen when the Japanese attacked Pearl Harbor, I watched the United States mobilize for war in a way that stunned the rest of the world. The Japanese had "awakened a sleeping giant," and the greatest manufacturing machine in the world came to life. As a result, to my generation, Industrial America was king–the king to which we eagerly pledged our talents, our efforts, our loyalties, and our lives.

When he came to Harvard, JF was the president and CEO of the company. His brother, J. C. Lincoln, had actually founded Lincoln Electric. Although JC was the technical genius behind their unique products and manufacturing system, JF had the vision.

During my interview, JF was open and direct. He asked pointed questions about my time in the army, my fraternity presidency (Nu Alpha Phi), and my ROTC and military records while at Pomona

College. (Fortunately, he didn't dwell on my football and track accomplishments).

To my surprise, out of all my successes up to that point, JF zeroed in on a summer job I had taken selling Fuller Brushes door-to-door in Los Angeles. During the Great Depression, I had seen all too well the effects of financial hardship. One Friday evening when I was nine, I watched my father ask our neighbor for ten dollars so we could buy groceries for the weekend. In that moment, I vowed never to be in my father's position. Ever. I held some sort of a job from that day on. Consequently, with my brown suitcase full of Fuller Brushes, I *ran* between the exclusive Los Feliz estates to increase the number of sales I could make.

JF seemed to be impressed by that.

At the close of the interview, he stated, "During the past twenty-five years, I have been able to cut manufacturing costs over 90 percent. I have not been able to reduce sales costs one bit. If you come to work for me, what will you do about that?"

I'm sure I said something brilliant, like "um" or "uh," stumbling for an answer. Whatever I said, it must have been enough as he invited me to visit his new factory in Cleveland. While I was there, he offered me a job. The training program was scheduled to start in June . . . in Lincoln's Welding School . . . in Cleveland.

I didn't take the job.

-3-

Blondes + Convertibles + California Sunshine = Trouble

A CALIFORNIA KID AT heart, I envisioned beginning my career overlooking the Pacific Ocean. After graduating from Harvard Business School, I drove my 1951 Plymouth from Boston to Chicago, then picked up the famous Route 66 to LA to look for a job. I had several offers in Southern California, including offers from Standard Oil and Carnation Milk. I even received an offer to become sales manager of Forest Lawn Cemetery.

However, I couldn't get J. F. Lincoln, his company, and his values out of my mind.

Needless to say, I didn't just sprout out of the ground in 1953. I shot into the world in Los Angeles in 1928, the second of three children. I landed between the end of the Roaring Twenties and the beginning of the Great Depression, when the world was moving from boom to bust and the greatest century in the history of mankind was just getting warmed up.

I was the kind of kid who hit the ground running and didn't stop until I hit the wall—or in my case, the wall hit *me*—but I'll go into that later.

Growing up in Southern California in those days, at least to me, was equivalent to growing up in paradise: glorious weather, little traffic, no pollution, the glamour of Hollywood, and the magnificent Pacific Ocean. There was no better place in the world to be a kid. Too bad it isn't that way anymore.

Between the Depression and WWII, there was a lot going on around me. In the 1930s, I'd watched people suffer, struggle, and lose hope. After the Japanese attacked Pearl Harbor in 1941, I witnessed an entire nation snap to attention and galvanize for war—a war that sparked patriotism, cooperation, ingenuity, loyalty, and hard work.

Because the West Coast was the next logical target for the Japanese after bombing the Hawaiian Islands, throughout the war, Southern California was a blackout area, with the bright lights of Hollywood all but extinguished. Everyone of Japanese descent, from Washington state to the border of Mexico, was forced into internment camps. The fact that some were US citizens made no difference. Everywhere we turned, Southern Californians were made all too aware that our country was at war.

As my dad traveled a lot and my mother refused to drive (which, it turned out, worked to my advantage), I got my driver's license at fourteen. At sixteen, my dad helped me buy my first car, a gorgeous five-year-old 1940 Mercury V-8 convertible, cream with red leather seats. Heaven. My dad wasn't thrilled with my choice (for obvious reasons), but since I was paying for half plus all expenses, he couldn't really force me to buy a more conservative car. He didn't even try.

When I entered high school, I was only 5'4" tall and weighed less than 120 pounds. At my size and weight, athletics, at least the ones I liked, were out of the question. The sports schedules also conflicted with my after-school jobs. Since the war was front and center on everyone's mind and I was too young to enlist, I joined the Junior ROTC. I stayed in ROTC throughout high school, and by my senior year, I'd obtained the rank of battalion adjutant, a captain.

My junior year I finally started to grow. By my senior year, I was 6'0" tall and weighed 150 pounds soaking wet–finally big enough for varsity football (barely). I was appointed backup quarterback.

About this time, a young lady named Carolyn entered my life. She was a junior and a startling blonde beauty. One afternoon, *I skipped football practice* to drive Carolyn along the beach in Santa Monica in my convertible. The ride took the entire afternoon.

Unbeknownst to me, while I was busy showing off in Santa Monica, the football coach had changed our entire offense, from a single-wing running attack to a T-formation passing game in preparation for an upcoming game against Hollywood High. Because I could throw the ball pretty well, our coach had decided I would be the new starting quarterback!

When I showed up for practice the next afternoon, the coach was livid. I had missed the practice of his new offense and was persona non grata. He kicked me off the team on the spot and told me to never show up for practice again. I was devastated. Here was my big chance and I blew it. I learned two important lessons that day:

1. Always show up.

2. Blondes + Convertibles + California Sunshine = Trouble.

I was barely seventeen when I graduated from Fairfax High School in Los Angeles in January 1946. (I told you I hit the ground running!) As the war ended, the GI Bill was still available for returning servicemen. I planned to join the army immediately after kissing Fairfax (and Carolyn, of course) good-bye and worry about college later. UCLA would still be there when I got back. However, my dad refused to sign the parental consent form for recruits under eighteen years of age until I first attended one semester of college. Left with little choice, I enrolled in Los Angeles City College. Although the classes were great, and I admit that I learned a few things, I still had my sights set on the army.

War leaves an indelible footprint.

After one semester at Los Angeles City College, Dad was good to his word and signed the waiver. I joined the army as a private at seventeen, just months before the war ended. Although the fighting had stopped, World War II was not officially declared over by Congress until December 1946. Consequently, I was considered a WWII veteran. I'd gotten in just under the wire.

After enlisting, I was sent by train to Fort Lewis, Washington, for basic training. I became an expert marksman with a Garand M1 .30-caliber rifle. After eight weeks, two thousand other new recruits and I were loaded onto a Victory Troop Ship called the *Pomona Victory* and we steamed west. I threw up all the way to Japan.

After two very long weeks, we landed in Yokohama. I was assigned to the Thirteenth Field Artillery Battalion of the Twenty-Fourth Infantry Division at Camp Hakata, near Fukuoka, on the southern island of Kyushu. We rode for three days and two nights on a train that reminded me of something out of the Wild West in the 1800s.

After a couple of weeks training to drive a two-and-a-half-ton truck, I was summoned to the battery commander's office and questioned about my driving abilities. I had just turned eighteen and apparently had impressed the commander with four years of licensed driving experience. I don't think my 135 Army Entrance Exam score hurt either (thank you, Fairfax High School and Los Angeles City College).

I was appointed the commander's personal Jeep driver and assigned my very own Jeep. What a deal!

Then I had an idea.

I just happened to be a wiz at detailing vehicles. I immediately wrote to my mother, asking her to send me a can of Simoniz (pronounced with a long *i*), the best car wax money could buy. She did, and my Jeep became the envy of the entire battalion. Unlike the war years, during peacetime, a flat finish, camouflaged vehicle wasn't necessary to avoid getting shot, so a shiny, polished Jeep was acceptable. My commander received a lot of attention and he loved every minute of it.

So did I.

Toward the end of 1947, some of our occupation forces were being sent back to the States. We were given a choice: we could tour the Philippines and Southeast Asia on a ship and possibly reenlist, or we could return to the United States with an early discharge.

I talked over my options with my battery commander. He told me straight out that he felt I had too much potential to stay in the army as an enlisted man. He recommended that I leave Japan as soon as possible, go to college, take ROTC, and become a commissioned officer.

That's exactly what I did. A commissioned officer has a much nicer lifestyle than an enlisted man.

I should know. I had driven them around Japan.

-4-

Pomona—Not Just a Victory Ship

I WAS DISCHARGED FROM the army on January 6, 1948, as a corporal (tech 5). When I arrived back in California, I showed my dad a photo of the *Pomona Victory* troop ship the army had given me. Without missing a beat, he said, "I understand there is a good college named Pomona about fifty miles from here. You should check it out."

I had never heard of it.

Two days later, Mom and I drove out to Claremont, California, and met with Pomona's dean of admissions. I liked the fact that it was a small school—I had a much better chance of playing sports. UCLA, the natural choice for someone from my socioeconomic background, was beyond my reach athletically and the only school within my reach financially—without the GI Bill. When the dean learned I was interested in business, he recommended that I look at Claremont Men's College next door (now Claremont-McKenna College).

"But Pomona is my destiny!" I replied stubbornly, flashing him the photo of my ship. (I failed to mention that a college that enrolled *women* was also my destiny.) He accepted me on the spot as a second semester freshman and helped me fill out the request for the GI Bill. I guess he liked my pitch. I started classes the following week.

Pomona actually did allow me join the football team my sophomore year. As a second semester freshman, I had missed the opportunity to play in the fall. I played for three years and was blessed to play one game in the famous Rose Bowl, in Pasadena, against Cal Tech.

It is rare that a man's greatest moments are immediately followed by his most humiliating, but in the game against Cal Tech, I managed to accomplish both in under 15 seconds.

That fateful night, there were only about one thousand fans in the one-hundred-thousand-seat stadium. It was eerie, akin to playing in a some sort of ghost stadium. I played safety. Late in the fourth quarter, Cal Tech was behind by seven points and needed a Hail Mary pass to tie the game. With under a minute to go, the quarterback threw long. Turning my head at the last second, I intercepted the desperation pass on our two-yard line. With my adrenaline on overdrive, I zigged and zagged my way up toward their goal line. I picked up some blockers and shot into the end zone for a spectacular ninety-eight-yard run. I threw my arms in the air to spike the football.

There was only one problem—I didn't have the ball. I had dropped it somewhere around the fifteen-yard line. In all my excitement, somehow this little fact had escaped my attention and I had kept right on running. (Pomona recovered the ball, thank God.) To add insult to injury, my parents happened to be in the stands that night. My mother told me later that Dad turned to her and announced, "MY son caught the ball, YOUR son dropped it." They never came to another game. (So much for my football career).

Due to my previous military service, in order to earn my commission, I was only required to enroll in the advanced ROTC courses for two years in lieu of the normal four. It paid a whopping $27.90 per month! During the summer of my second year, I was sent back to Fort Lewis for six weeks of intensive training. Fort Lewis had 1200 cadets from the eleven western states.

Shortly after I arrived, I overheard two lieutenants talking about the cadets. They mentioned that they were looking for cadets who were imaginative and showed initiative—not just those who followed orders.

Hmmmmm.

Then I had an idea.

In Japan, I had learned a special way of folding socks to keep my footlocker different and distinctive. Since I was one of a select few cadets who had prior military experience, I hoped this little trick might get me noticed.

Surprisingly, it did. All the way up the ladder.

Soon after, on the evening before our M1 rifle inspection, I asked our barracks sergeant if we were to prepare for a regular or dry inspection. He replied, "dry," which in military speak means *no oil*.

Then I had another idea.

If you've never cleaned an M1, it's a painstaking process and it's next to impossible to clean the weapon completely. That night, while the other cadets were cleaning their rifles, I decided to treat myself to a trip to the beer hall. As I left the barracks and headed for a little libation, I could hear the other cadets mumbling that I was a crazy SOB who obviously harbored some sort of bizarre death wish. I just smiled.

Early the next morning, before the bugler blew his first note, I got up, grabbed my rifle, and carried it into the shower with me. I rigorously cleaned both of us with soap and *very* hot water. The M1 was steaming by the time I got out. As the water evaporated and the weapon cooled, I dressed quickly. With under a minute to spare, I grabbed my rifle and raced into formation.

The inspecting lieutenant took one look at my weapon and muttered, "What the hell."

Before he could bark at me, I blurted out, "My sergeant told us it was a *dry inspection*, SIR."

He just shook his head, rolled his eyes, and went on to the next cadet.

Once we were dismissed, I raced back to the barracks and oiled my rifle. I was lucky that the lieutenant hadn't made me stand on the pavement until it rusted.

I raised the bar on everything I could think of to stand out. Since military life is extremely structured and limited in the "opportunities to be creative" department, my efforts were all very simple yet distinctive enough to be noticed.

As a direct result of these efforts, at the end of the training I was awarded the top medal. I was first out of a class of 1,200—all dressed identically, with identical haircuts and identical equipment. Upon returning to Pomona, I was promoted to cadet colonel, commander of our ROTC unit.

In June 1950, at the end of my junior year, I received my second lieutenant's commission. I volunteered for a summer tour as a basic training instructor at Fort Ord, California, home of the Fourth Infantry Division, near Monterey and Carmel (tough assignment).

I arrived at Fort Ord on June 20. On June 25, the North Koreans attacked South Korea. The camp all but imploded! Within a week, ALL OFFICERS except the base commander and second lieutenant Donald Hastings were shipped to the Korean peninsula. Apparently, since I was a volunteer, the army had skipped over me.

Whew!

All summer long I trained reservists. All we were able to do to prepare them for what lay ahead was to give them a worn-out rifle from WWII (that's all we had), a couple of hours on the rifle range and the infiltration course, and two or three medical shots. Within a week of their arrival at Fort Ord, the reservists were on their way to Korea. It was awful.

Although all these guys were WWII veterans and had, at some point, completed basic training, many had never seen combat. During the war, a vast number had been cooks, drivers or had served in the supply corps. They were ill-prepared for what lay ahead.

I don't know how they did it, but this motley crew of brave Americans held on to the tip of the Pusan peninsula until General Douglas McArthur landed with fresh, highly trained Camp Pendleton troops at Inchon, behind North Korean lines–a brilliant maneuver. Those guys all deserved a medal.

Toward the end of the summer, while still at Fort Ord, I was summoned to the commander's office. He informed me that because there were so few army volunteers, Congress hadn't felt it was necessary to pass a bill to hold them (he meant me) on active duty. Translation: the army required my signature to hold me for the duration of the "conflict." The commander tried every trick in the book, including promising to *try* to keep me at Fort Ord, to entice me to sign.

I was shocked. Here I was, sitting in a commander's office on an army base, wearing an infantry uniform with a second lieutenant's bar and crossed rifles pinned on my collar, training men for battle during an armed "conflict." Given the severity of the situation, it had *never occurred to me* that I was not committed to continuous military service for the duration of the conflict.

As I listened to him prattle on, it slowly dawned on me that my volunteer status might afford me the opportunity to leave Fort Ord and finish my college career. I told him I'd think it over. I called our regular army ROTC officer at Pomona and explained the situation.

"Don't sign ANYTHING!" he barked. "Come back to school and join a reserve unit. It is far better to go into a war as part of a unit or team. You *don't* want to go over there as an infantry replacement officer. *You know* what happens to them."

It didn't take a stroke of genius to know I didn't want to go to Korea (or anywhere else, for that matter) as an infantry replacement. I had watched them all summer and I knew what they faced.

Instead, I joined the 399th Military Police Battalion in Pasadena. It was a vibrant command of military veterans, most of whom were active police officers in Southern California. I spent about two years as part of this battalion, changing my branch from infantry to military police. Our unit was never called. After witnessing the postwar devastation in Japan, I must admit I wasn't sorry we were never called to active duty. Although I had never been there, I was sure I would always prefer Pasadena, California, to the Pusan peninsula in Korea.

I graduated from Pomona in 1951 with academic honors. I also carried the title of Distinguished Military Graduate.

-5-

"Uncle!"

AFTER SIX WEEKS in Los Angeles looking for a job, I finally yelled "Uncle!" J. F. Lincoln's voice and message had been playing in my head in a never-ending, highly annoying loop. With a huge sigh, I realized I would be leaving California.

But . . . *Cleveland?* I had just survived my first two winters in Boston and had no desire to repeat the experience. I was still programmed for sun-drenched days and sun-kissed blondes.

However, that little voice in my head had turned to a dull roar. Yes, Lincoln Electric . . . and Cleveland. I called Buck Persons, the vice president of sales at Lincoln, to ask him if the job was still open. It was. In fact, the training program had already started.

Then I had an idea.

Before I hung up the phone I asked, "At the end of training, any possibility I can be sent to Los Angeles?"

With no hesitation whatsoever, he said, "Sure." I had no idea that Buck had already decided to leave Lincoln to become president of Emerson Electric in St. Louis. I could have asked him to send me to the moon after training and he would have said, "No problem."

On my first day at Lincoln, I drove up to a big gray building in Euclid, Ohio, World Headquarters of the Lincoln Electric Company. There wasn't a window in sight. (Soon after, I found out there weren't any—*at all*.) As I walked through the glass doors and down the staircase, I read the slogan on the wall:

"The Actual Is Limited, The Possible Is Immense."

Wow, I thought. I've come to the right place. I couldn't wait to start my new career. I hurried down the tunnel to the welding school.

Sometime during those first few months buried in the bowels of the company, I was called into the personnel office. Since I had been hired by JF personally (and was a late arrival), I hadn't been processed through the proper channels. They asked me to fill out an application. The last question addressed my future: What is your long-term goal at Lincoln? Without hesitation, I wrote, "President." It wasn't until many years later that I realized I had shot low.

As the training program wound to a close, I kept telling anyone and everyone within earshot that I was going to be sent to Los Angeles. Finally, Jack Roscoe, Buck's successor, called me into his office and asked me flat out if going to Los Angeles had been a condition of my employment. It was, of course, in *my* mind, and I told him so. Since Buck had obviously not informed anyone of our previous conversation, Jack had no way to confirm my story. Fortunately, he took me at my word. Several weeks later, Jack told me I had been slotted for the San Francisco Bay office in Emeryville, California.

Close enough.

-6-

I Found My Heart in
San Francisco

FROM MY FIRST night in the Bay Area, my life began to change. First, Charlie Stocker, the manager of the Northern California office, invited me home for dinner. Second, my best friend from Pomona, Gurnee Hart, informed me that Shirley Tedder, "Teddy," also a Pomona classmate, was living in Berkeley. Shirley and I had gone to one dance together at Pomona, but nothing had come of it. We'd had a really nice evening, but since, at the time, we were both still smarting from recent breakups, neither one of us had felt any sparks. As they say, timing is everything.

Shirley had decided against falling into the traditional role of teacher or nurse. To everyone's surprise, she had bravely walked away from a graduate program in teaching at the University of California, Berkeley (in an "aha" moment as a student teacher, she had suddenly realized that she disliked teaching). Shirley then proceeded to take the civil service exam and shocked the board by scoring the highest marks of anyone taking the test. Consequently, she had been hired by the Juvenile Division of the Berkeley Police Department. Our Teddy was a cop!

(Well, actually, she held a special position as a juvenile police officer, working with the school system and the juvenile courts, but that's not as much fun to say.)

Shirley was also an active member of the Northern California Juvenile Officers Association and even designed the logos for both that organization and the California Juvenile Officers Association. To this day, Shirl hates it when I call her a cop—although our daughters swear she can search a room as well as any forensic specialist on the planet.

Never one to hesitate to spend an evening with a beautiful woman, I called Teddy, reintroduced myself, and asked if I could stop by after my dinner with Charlie. She said, "Yes, but I hope you don't mind, I'll be washing my hair." (I told you there hadn't been any sparks.) I didn't mind. I had a sister. I spent the entire evening regaling her with tales of Lincoln Electric and its fabulous values and philosophy. Looking back, I marvel at the fact that she didn't write me off then and there as some kind of overzealous lunatic.

I was hooked: that night on Lincoln Electric, and soon after, on Shirley.

-7-

A Funny Little Welding Company in Euclid, Ohio

($60 million in sales when I joined, $1.25 billion when I left)

BEFORE I GO any further into the scintillating details of my early career, perhaps I should mention why a California-born Harvard MBA chose to join a little known company in a dirty industry located in the Rust Belt of the United States—an industry where I'd have to wear a *welding mask* to do my job.

The Lincoln Electric Company, based in Euclid, Ohio, is truly unique. In fact, it has been a case study at Harvard Business School for sixty-five years. In 2015, Lincoln will mark its 120th anniversary.

In 1895, with only a few hundred dollars and a great idea, John C. Lincoln founded what would one day become a Fortune 500 company. He was a brilliant engineer from Ohio State University and a first-class entrepreneur. By 1914, when his younger brother, James F. Lincoln, joined the organization, JC already owned numerous patents and had begun the production of electric motors.

Although JC was an electrical genius, JF was magnetic. He immediately began to implement new and progressive ideas into the company. In fact, JF's charisma and unique philosophies are what had so attracted me to Lincoln in the first place. It certainly hadn't been welding and it *most* certainly hadn't been Cleveland.

JF had begun his tenure with the company by appointing an advisory board of employees to assist him. The advisory board was somewhat similar to the employee representative programs (ERPs) of the times. Those in power in Washington believed the existence of ERPs would block or retard the entrance of national unions into many large and well-established companies. In 1935, in order to promote national unions, ERPs were declared illegal by the Wagner Act. However, because Lincoln employees did not bargain for wages during their advisory board meetings, they were exempt from this law.

In addition, JF instituted a unique open-door policy, giving any employee permission to come into his office to speak with him about any aspect of his employment or working conditions. I am not sure if this policy is honored today. It would be a shame if it were not. Although living in a fishbowl can be trying at times, open communication can provide a wealth of otherwise unobtainable information and forge irreplaceable bonds between labor and management.

In 1915, Lincoln implemented a "piece work" system on the factory floor. Instead of paying hourly wages, the company paid workers on the amount of quality work they completed. This type of system was quite prevalent at the turn of the nineteenth century. However, because greedy managers took advantage of the system by cutting a worker's "piece rate" whenever they began earning too much money, the system gradually faded away.

JF, on the other hand, guaranteed a worker's rates would remain constant unless a significant change was made in the worker's production process. The end result of this system is that workers have an incentive to become more productive as increased productivity leads to a direct increase in their earnings. Consequently, Lincoln factory workers work harder, smarter, and more efficiently than the typical hourly employee. As a result, they are among the most highly paid factory workers in the world. They also trust management not to cut their rates unfairly.

In addition, JF began a profit sharing plan, equivalent to about 35 percent of net profits. The money was traditionally distributed annually on the first Friday in December. (The retail establishments in greater Cleveland salivate at bonus time!) Although many companies have profit sharing plans, I know of very few who consistently share such a large percentage with ALL their employees, not merely upper management. Because of the high percentage payout, quite a few factory personnel commute over two hours for the opportunity to work and participate. Keeping in mind that Lincoln is located in a snowbelt, this fact speaks volumes.

In opposition to many other types of programs, the Lincoln bonus is not equally distributed between employees. Each employee is merit-rated by their supervisor in a number of areas. Depending on the merit rating, dollar amounts can vary by as much as 20–30 percent for individual workers. Much like the game of golf, workers are in fierce competition with themselves. It is up to each individual to find ways to become more productive at his or her specific job. However, cooperation is also a key ingredient and is one of the primary merit-rating factors. Employees are encouraged to work both individually and cooperatively to increase the profitability of the company. Money is a terrific motivator for creativity, productivity, and cooperation. In fact, in my opinion, it is the preeminent motivator.

(If you want the best from your people, pay them what they are worth. If you want to know what they're worth, develop a program that will allow them to show you. Once they've shown you, pay up. Everybody wins.)

In 1958, Lincoln adopted a policy of *guaranteed employment*. After two years of service, no one could be laid off for economic reasons. Workers are guaranteed to be employed for at least 75 percent of a normal work week, or thirty of the normal forty hours. In exchange, during prosperous times, the employees agree to work mandatory overtime and accept job reassignments when necessary. During extremely busy times, fifty-four-hour work weeks are not uncommon. Overtime, of course, is paid over forty hours.

Both J. C. and J. F. Lincoln were deeply religious men, the sons of a Congregationalist minister. They believed in the Golden Rule–*do unto others as you would have them do unto you*–and treated their employees and customers accordingly. In addition to their unique production and management philosophies, their deep commitment to their employees is one of the main reasons I was drawn to Lincoln in the first place. Since I was raised under similar principles, we were a marriage made in heaven–just ask my wife.

The company now has more than forty manufacturing sites in about twenty countries around the world and is presently performing quite profitably in what is considered by many to be a sunset industry– of only $10–12 billion.

-8-

Open Up That
Golden Gate

WHILE I WAS excited to be back in my native California, I soon realized that my new boss, Charlie Stocker, had assigned me a territory the size of Australia—or so it seemed. My new sales territory ranged from Oakland and San Leandro, over to the San Joaquin Valley, all the way up to Redding then down to Fresno, including Sacramento, Stockton, Modesto, and Reno, Nevada (like I said, Australia).

To upgrade my technical expertise, Charlie "strongly suggested" I take some engineering courses at University of California, Berkeley, night school. Even with all my training, I guess my boss figured a liberal arts graduate with a BA in economics and an MBA in marketing wouldn't be of much use in a technical sales situation. I also think he was a little afraid I might electrocute myself. (Although I hate to admit it, he was probably right.) Today, the company primarily hires graduate engineers for the sales program—a very wise decision.

If you don't have a map, suffice it to say that I had the same number of accounts as other salesmen, but mine were spread out all over

Northern California and into Nevada. Bear in mind that there were no freeways in those days and air-conditioning in automobiles was a luxury I hadn't even considered. Contrary to popular opinion, parts of Northern California can be an oven in the summer, and I could see from day one that I was destined to spend my life in my car. It seemed to me that whoever had decided on the geographic boundaries of my newly acquired territory had never bothered to read the scale on the map. "Next town over" when you are west of the Mississippi River, and especially when you are west of the Rocky Mountains, takes on a whole new meaning.

How on earth was one guy supposed to cover all this ground by himself? To make matters worse, technical sales demanded that I have one-on-one contact with my accounts on a regular basis. The sheer size of my territory made this almost impossible.

Then I had an idea.

There were three major welding distributorships in my territory: Moore's Welding Supply in Sacramento, California Welding Supply in Stockton, and Middleton Welders Supply in San Leandro.

Unfortunately, my training in Cleveland had not included any tips on dealing with distributors. In fact, welding supply companies were most often referred to as "those damn dealers." In management's eyes, distributors were not an asset; they were an expense. The discount the dealers received from Lincoln cut into the company's profit margins, and the prevailing attitude at that time was that distributors were a necessary nuisance.

To make matters worse, there were hold-out lists. Within most contracts between manufacturers and dealers, the manufacturers would present lists of customers to the dealers that they were forbidden to solicit. The large accounts were commonly handled directly by the manufacturers. In essence, the manufacturers were cherry-picking customers, eating into the profit potential of their distributors. Needless to say, these practices did not lead to warm and fuzzy relationships.

I wanted to change all that.

Due to Lincoln's attitude toward dealers in general, I was completely taken by surprise by the degree of knowledge and professionalism displayed by some of these companies. Driving over thirty thousand miles per year had quickly taught me that I could use some help. I knew these guys knew the territory and knew the customers.

Toward the end of my first year in the field, JF stopped by our office on his way to Australia (the real Australia). Never one to pass up an opportunity to go to the top, I bent his ear about the value of the Welding Supply Distributor in widespread territories and presented him with my plan to utilize them to increase overall sales. To my surprise (and delight), he delayed his trip.

I dragged JF to both Moore's in Sacramento and California Welding Supply in Stockton. I must admit, I loved the extra time I had with him in the car. By the time we had visited both companies (and I had talked his ear off for the better part of a day), he had agreed to a trial program as long as the distributors were *treated fairly*. In his eyes, the Golden Rule was paramount to the success of anything.

After receiving JF's blessing, the first thing I did was to get rid of the hold-out lists and turn a number of my direct accounts over to the dealers. They were thrilled! I kept the accounts that were near the office and my home as I could service them properly on a direct basis. I also pushed Lincoln to expand the number of product lines our dealers were allowed to sell. JF agreed. This two-pronged approached enabled the dealers to service their customers more completely and increased their bottom lines substantially.

I worked very hard to change the way Lincoln viewed its dealers and even harder to change how my dealers viewed Lincoln—and me. Within two years, sales doubled in my territory. In 1957, Jack Roscoe, then vice president of sales, informed me that I had become the number two salesman in dollar volume in the country. Even more surprising to Jack was that I had accomplished that feat in a light manufacturing area.

I am convinced that I never could have accomplished such a high sales volume on my own selling direct. I was lucky that JF had been willing to listen to me in the first place. Looking back, I can see that JF had been keeping a watchful eye on my activities. The fact that he'd hired me directly probably had something to do with his interest.

-9-

Never Underestimate
the Power of Ice Cream

IT IS MY belief that people buy from people, not just companies, and they tend to buy from people they like. Successful selling is not only about solving problems but also, more importantly, about building relationships. I worked diligently to build solid relationships with all my customers and dealers. In fact, I treated my dealers as customers, which they were.

One of my biggest challenges as a new technical representative came from a call I made on International Harvester in Stockton, California. During the Korean conflict, there had been a steel shortage in the country, during which Lincoln had experienced difficulties buying enough steel for our electrode division. Consequently, some of our customers had experienced severe shortages. The International Harvester factory in Stockton was one of them.

Walt Foster had been the purchasing agent during the shortages, and as luck would have it, he was still there. He harbored a real grudge against Lincoln for not supplying Harvester during the conflict. On my first sales call, he really let me have it. Walt must have gone on for over a half hour and the longer he talked, the madder he got. The fact that I hadn't been with Lincoln during those years was irrelevant. No amount of technical expertise was going to get me out of hot water with Walt. (I learned later that I had not been the only salesman forced to lay my head on Walt's guillotine.)

During my dressing down, I happened to notice that Walt had a number of personal photos scattered around his office. Anxious to change the subject, I asked him about his background and family. When he finally calmed down, he told me about his son, a track star at the College of the Pacific (COP).

The next time I called on him, about two weeks later, Walt had simmered down—a little. At least he seemed to be a little less belligerent. To keep him off the subject of Lincoln, shortages, and me, I steered the conversation toward his son, the up-and-coming track star. Walt mentioned that he was going to watch his son run in the Modesto Relays the following Saturday and that he, Walt, would be manning the ice cream stand. Although we had a rather pleasant chat about Walt's son, it was clear to me that I still had a long way to go to earn Walt's business.

Then I had an idea.

I called Shirley and asked if she would like to drive out to the Valley to watch a track meet the following Saturday. I was offering her the opportunity to enjoy a long boring drive, the chance to root for a complete stranger at a track meet in order to impress a Lincoln customer she'd never met, and a long boring drive back. I couldn't believe she didn't jump at the chance to join me. After employing all my best sales skills, I finally persuaded her to go. To this day she tells me she thought I was nuts. Motivated, yes—even inspired, perhaps—but nuts.

That fateful Saturday we spent a total of five hours driving back and forth to Modesto in my 1951 Plymouth, baked in the sun for far too long, watched Walt's son run around the track a few times, cheered like crazy for a kid we didn't know, and ate enough ice cream to make us ill.

I got the order . . . and many, many more. My experience with Walt taught me a lot about the value of personal selling: _there is no substitute_.

-10-

The Kitchen
Confrontation

WHEN I FIRST moved to the Bay Area, I rented a room in the basement of a home in the Berkeley Hills for $25.00 a month. Because of the size of my territory, I often left home on Sunday evening in order to be able to see customers early Monday morning–the adult equivalent of running between houses, selling Fuller Brush. On Friday night, I would drive back to Berkeley to have dinner with Shirley.

Since I often arrived back late, dinner wasn't until about 9:00 p.m. More times than not, Shirley would cook for the two of us. Between my enthusiasm for Lincoln, a cheap room, and free meals, I had a really good thing going. I would regale Shirley with tales of my travels, mesmerizing her with my sales and technical prowess (or so she let me believe). At the stroke of midnight, after Jan Pierce sang "Bluebird of Happiness" on the radio, Shirl would usher me out. We must have repeated this scenario at least seven or eight times before I got up the nerve to steal a good-night kiss.

On more than one occasion, I showed up at Shirl's suffering "weld flashes," the result of accidental exposure to the welding arc without proper eye protection. My eyes were the color of rubies and the burning sensation was, shall I say, *invigorating*. Shirl was very patient with me and spent many an evening cutting raw potato slices for my eyes (the accepted remedy for my particular ailment). I don't believe potatoes are covered under worker's comp. They should be. As she gently applied the potatoes, I continued chatting excitedly about my escapades all across Northern California. What a Don Juan I was in those days.

One evening, after this routine had been going on for several months, Shirl verbally accosted me in the kitchen. (Remember—she was a cop!)

"Donald, where is this heading? I'm twenty-four years old, and unless you're interested in this relationship moving forward, I'm outta here" (or words to that effect). "If you're not serious, then quit eating my food and wasting my time."

Huh?

I was stunned. I didn't know what to say or do. I knew I had a really good thing going—an appreciative audience, an attentive "nurse" of sorts, and a free meal or two every week with a beautiful woman. Frankly, I was perfectly content to ride that wave as long as I could. In fact, up until that moment, I'd never really given the situation much thought.

MY life was great. (Typical male, I know.)

So I did the only reasonable thing a man in my position could do: I finished eating my dinner. This little incident has come to be known in the Hastings family as the Kitchen Confrontation. I was the salesman, but obviously I was not the only one in the room who was not afraid to ask for an order.

In retrospect, Shirley's challenge was the beginning of a new chapter in my life, one that I am still writing today. Her ultimatum was a key turning point. The world had really begun to change for me, but until that infamous Kitchen Confrontation, I was under the mistaken impression that I still had options.

Until my mother got involved.

One weekend, shortly after the notorious "confrontation," my parents were visiting the Bay Area. I introduced them to Shirley and we had a wonderful evening. Dad fell in love with her, and I was perfectly happy with how my life was progressing.

Then Mom had an idea.

Walking back from a Mort Sahl performance in San Francisco, my mother, a 4'10" spitfire, poked me in the ribs with her elbow, pointed to Shirley, and said, "Marry that girl."

I did.

-11-

A Room with a View

A YEAR OR SO after we were married, the Moore brothers offered me a job. They were planning to open a new dealership in San Francisco and wanted me to run it. The opportunity would have given me eventual ownership in the company and I would have been guaranteed a life in California. Wow.

Shirley had no problem staying in the Bay Area. Why would she? Our apartment in El Cerrito overlooked San Francisco Bay. The view was spectacular (until the fog rolled in and swallowed everything up). When that happened during the summer, we would take road trips to Macy's in San Francisco to laugh at the tourists buying coats.

In those days I did my taxes while sitting at our dining room table, gazing out across the windswept bay, the glorious Golden Gate Bridge, and down on a lonely little island called Alcatraz. In the 1950s, Alcatraz was a fully operational federal maximum-security prison, boasting quite a guest list. Shirl and I would watch the boats motoring back and forth across the bay, carrying supplies. I can hardly believe that Alcatraz is now a tourist attraction. In our era, very few ventured to that compound *voluntarily*. Looking out on that island, with its gloomy gray buildings, high concrete walls, barbed wire fencing, and shark-infested waters, I'm sure I overpaid my taxes.

After further discussions with Charlie (my boss), my dad and Gurnee Hart's dad about the Moore brothers' offer, I decided to fly to Cleveland at my own expense to talk to Jack Roscoe. Roscoe suggested I speak directly with JF, probably because JF had hired me. JF's question to me was simple: "Do you want to be a big fish in a small pond or a big fish in a big pond?"

I turned down Moore's offer.

Shortly thereafter, I was offered the Lincoln district manager's position in Minneapolis, which included both North and South Dakota. Coincidence? I don't believe in coincidences. My dad's only comment was, "Keep in mind, it's colder than Boston."

I turned it down.

Looking back, I can't believe I refused that offer. Shirl and I, as native Californians, just couldn't envision ourselves locked away in the Cold White North. I'm lucky I didn't derail my entire career over the climate.

Although I didn't think about it much, by Lincoln standards, I was somewhat of a renegade. I was young, brash, and unpredictable–and I was not afraid to make mistakes. I was constantly coming up with new ideas not only because I wanted to get noticed, but also because my mind just worked that way. It always has.

The Bethlehem Steel plant on the island of Alameda was one of my favorite accounts. Bethlehem Steel built the Golden Gate Bridge (1934–1937). They had supplied both the steel and the labor. When I called on them, they were using our twin-arc process mounted on a standard overhead carriage. Although they liked the setup, it was immobile: the beams had to be brought to the welding operation. Bethlehem wanted it to be the other way around.

No problem, right?

In a flash of either genius or lunacy (I'm not sure which), I persuaded them to buy a Lincoln submerged arc tractor and I set out to retrofit our twin-arc system to fit their requirements. On a wing and a prayer, I designed and built the unit in their repair shop. To everyone's amazement (including my own), it worked!

I loved my job. I was running all over Northern California, trying new things and finding unique and creative ways to solve problems. Fortunately, most of them worked. But I really didn't care one way or the other–I was having a ball! I looked at every so-called problem as an *opportunity to be creative*, and I became a "Thank God, it's Monday" guy. Driving my 1955 Ford V-8 Coupe at 112 miles an hour made the miles fly by. (I failed to mention to Shirley that I occasionally drove that fast–on dark, unlit, two-lane roads with no lines, multiple curves and the possibility of driving up the back of a poorly illuminated tractor-trailer at breakneck speeds.)

After rereading that sentence, I'm glad I had daughters.

-12-

Quad Cities, USA:
The Corn Belt

AFTER FIVE YEARS in the Bay Area, Jack Roscoe offered me the district manager's position in Moline, Illinois. Shirley and I could barely find Moline on the map! As my father was a native of Iowa and my mother a native of Illinois, my parents blessed the move and off we went. Shirley had left the police department and was six months pregnant with our first daughter, Leslie Anne.

Since the University of Iowa's football team, the Hawkeyes, had played in the Rose Bowl in Pasadena just two days prior to my scheduled arrival in the Midwest, all flights into the Quad Cities were booked for weeks. Apparently, instead of returning home immediately following the game to a frigid winter (it was January, after all), the fans were taking their time enjoying the California sunshine. Who could blame them?

I hopped on a train and headed east.

When I left Berkeley on January 3, the temperature was a balmy sixty-eight degrees. Three days later, I stepped off the train in Savanna, Illinois—temperature minus-thirteen degrees! I bought a coat, hat, and gloves before I left the train station—or at least I would have if they'd been available back then. Train stations and airports have come a long way.

Within a few days of my arrival, the temperature had risen to a blistering ZERO and I flew back to California to pick up Shirl. We drove back to Illinois in our much-loved white 1958 Plymouth convertible (yes, the one with the big fins). Little did we know it would be a long time before we would be able to put the top down again.

Upon arriving in Moline, we discovered that there was a mover's strike in process. Consequently, our furniture couldn't be delivered and we were forced to rent a furnished apartment. All we could find on short notice was a basement unit with less than five hundred square feet and, we found out quickly, a rather questionable heating system. To this day Shirl has never forgiven me for sticking her in a freezing basement with no friends. From the way she occasionally looked at me back then, I could have sworn the temperature in the room dropped even further.

Right before Leslie was born, we moved into a small rental house in Davenport, Iowa, across the Mississippi River from Moline. We later bought a house not far from there.

Although Moline was a city of only forty thousand, Deere & Company was headquartered just outside town and had four factories inside the city limits. It also had multiple other locations scattered across Iowa in Ottumwa, Des Moines, and Waterloo. J. I. Case had facilities in Bettendorf and Burlington, Iowa, and International Harvester had plants in East Moline and Rock Island, Illinois. In three short days, I had been transported from a land of infinite variety to the very heart of the farm equipment capital of the planet.

The Quad Cities consists of Moline, East Moline, and Rock Island, Illinois, and Davenport, Iowa. The Mississippi River runs right through them. The Lincoln District Office included two suboffices in Cedar Rapids and Des Moines, Iowa. This area of America uses a great deal of arc welding, and I was about to dive headfirst into the Breadbasket of the World.

Just before I'd left California, I'd had the good fortune to call on Blackwelder Manufacturing Company in Rio Vista. They introduced me to a new process, gas-shielded semiautomatic welding, or MIG (metal inert gas) welding manufactured by Airco, one of our competitors. The superintendent was really excited about the new process and, horror of horrors, Blackwelder was replacing our product, Jetweld, with MIG. Little did I know that upon arriving in the Quad Cities, I would find the entire Midwest moving in the same direction! It was as if a big black cloud had followed me across the country.

To add insult to injury, Lincoln management was not even remotely interested in hearing about this new technology, let alone doing anything about it. I had left my beloved California, traveled over two thousand miles to a place Shirley and I could barely find on a map, and dumped my very pregnant wife in a frigid basement, friendless, only to find myself thrashing around in a salesman's nightmare! At that moment, I wondered how far the temperature actually dropped in Minneapolis. It couldn't be THAT much colder there.

To give you an idea of the disaster I walked into, I need to get a little technical. The farm equipment business is a "natural" for gas-shielded arc welding (MIG). At the time of my arrival in the Midwest, in 1959, Lincoln's 3/16" Fleetweld 7 (E-6012) was the major stick electrode used in the area. However, we were rapidly losing market share to the MIG process. MIG welding—with its many small intermittent welds (many made out of position), no slag removal, and higher operating factors than conventional stick welding—enabled our customers to lower costs. In short, MIG welding was a faster and lower-cost way to weld these products. Our longtime customers were leaving Lincoln in droves, heading straight for the competition.

Wow.

Welcome to the Quad Cities, Don.

-13-

John Deere and the
Silver-Tongued
Mesmerist

JOHN DEERE WAS a longtime loyal Lincoln customer. In fact, Deere & Company was the reason the Moline District Office had been opened in the first place.

Although the John Deere plants were unionized, they did employ a piecework system of sorts on the shop floors. Contrary to the Lincoln system, workers were given a daily quota. However, they were not paid extra if they surpassed it. Consequently, in an eight-hour shift, some workers finished their work in as little as six hours. As employees were not allowed to leave early, they were actually allowed to kill time until the day was officially over—an odd, but fairly common practice in those days.

The actual welding time was based on using Lincoln's Fleetweld 7, and extra time was allotted for slag removal (very slow slag removal, I noticed). Switching over to MIG would require recalculating all the piece rates due to a change in process. At least I had one thing working in my favor: recalculating piece rates is no small feat. Although corporate was pushing the new MIG process to cut costs, I was running around in circles trying to prevent it.

Then I had an idea.

To combat the influx of MIG, the entire office began pushing Lincoln's new Innershield product, in which the flux is inside the tubular steel rather that coated on the outside of a solid rod as it is on stick electrode. To our detriment, although Innershield was continuous, it did carry slag and couldn't produce the small welds available with MIG.

We did have some success with Innershield at John Deere Plow and John Deere Dubuque and a little more at John Deere Des Moines, thanks to Lee Allgood, who covered Des Moines for Lincoln. However, when it came to welding thinner-grade metals, Lincoln couldn't compete. We did not offer Innershield in small enough diameters, and even if we had, it left a slag that had to be chipped off.

As all this nonsense was occurring, I kept promising Deere that we were working on a new product that would be on the market in short order. I'm surprised my nose didn't grow right in front of the plant manager. I was scrambling to buy time. I knew that once Deere switched over to MIG with a competitor, it would be next to impossible to convert them back to a Lincoln process. Once large companies make a significant change, they tend to stay with it—for obvious reasons. I did everything in my power to stall Deere from a changeover to MIG, but I knew time was not on my side. I was quickly running out of tricks up my sleeve.

Finally, the corporate Powers That Be at Deere headquarters had enough of the stalling and put in a call to John Deere Ottumwa: "Stop listening to that *Silver-Tongued Mesmerist!* We are converting to gas shielding NOW and we don't want to hear another word about it!"

They were referring to me.

I caught wind of the conversation from my friends in the plant and the name stuck. To this day, I've never managed to live it down. (Actually, I've secretly spent my life trying to live UP to it.)

Lincoln management ignored our pleas and flat out refused to meet the competition head-on (or *at all*). "Lincoln is not in the gas business," they announced. What they meant was: *nor do we intend to be*. For some reason, they detested using gas to shield the arc even though one of J. C. Lincoln's early patents was for that precise process.

Someday, in Lincoln heaven, I hope I run into either JC or JF so I can ask them what this resistance was all about (not that my version of heaven is filled with Lincoln employees or anything).

I started losing business left and right.

-14-

A Motor Is a Motor
Is a Motor

IN THE EARLY 1960s, less than 10 percent of Lincoln's overall domestic sales volume came from our electric motor line. Welding machines and related products made up the other 90+ percent. Electric motors are a relatively simple product, with less engineering and manufacturing expertise required to produce the finished product.

However, since motors were J. C. Lincoln's first patented products and we still made a decent profit with them, the company continued to produce and market electric motors. The only interruption in our motor production had occurred during WWII, when welding machines were in such high demand to build the ships and tanks required to win the war, all motor-manufacturing facilities were converted to the production of welding equipment.

After several years of living the sales nightmare that was the Midwest (and having my lunch eaten by gas-shielded welding), I called Jack Roscoe in Cleveland. I told him I thought the Moline District Office should downsize in personnel to match our declining sales. I didn't really believe that, but I thought my comment would catch his attention.

It did.

With no hesitation, he barked, "Sell motors!"

Good God! What a ridiculous answer to a serious competitive threat! With Jack's inane comment I almost quit on the spot. (Did I mention motors represented only *ten percent* of our overall business?)

As luck would have it, Morris B. Pendleton, owner and CEO of Pendleton Tool Industries in Southern California, had recently contacted me with an offer to become his assistant. His son John and I had been classmates at both Pomona College and Harvard Business School. The offer sounded better than good considering Jack's response—added to the fact that the temperature in the Quad Cities had not crept above zero the entire month of January that year.

I contacted my dad for advice. I told him the facts. He said quietly, "You seem to be doing OK where you are. I think you should stay with Lincoln and see what happens." If it had not been for my complete faith in JF's ability to comprehend and overcome the impossible situation the company faced in the Midwest, I would have left in a heartbeat.

I followed Jack's orders and for the next six months hardly did anything but try to sell motors throughout our territory. All the tech reps made a heroic effort, but of course, we were not nearly successful enough to offset the losses to gas-shielded welding. However, by making this ridiculous attempt, I gained an interest in the motor industry as a whole and never dismissed it as inconsequential.

As my territory was slowly decimated by MIG welding, Lincoln remained deaf to my pleas. Obviously, motors couldn't save me. I wanted to get out of the Quad Cities before my career stalled completely. I looked around for other ways to get noticed.

Then I had an idea.

Lincoln held a district sales managers' meeting every year in Cleveland. Most of the speakers were from the large offices in major metropolitan areas. Not wanting to be overlooked simply because my offices were off the beaten track, I volunteered to be a speaker at as many meetings as I could. I was desperate and I took every opportunity to steal the spotlight. In those days we didn't have PowerPoint; we had flipcharts. Shirley, an art major at Pomona College, did a superb job of producing unique and clever slides and presentations. I practiced my talks in front of my daughters, and to this day, all three can quote Vince Lombardi verbatim.

It worked.

-15-

CAT

AFTER FOUR YEARS of fighting a losing battle to gas-shielded welding in the farm equipment industry, Frank Boucher, our new vice president of sales in Cleveland, asked me to meet him at the Pere Marquette Hotel in Peoria, Illinois. Caterpillar Tractor, the world's largest manufacturer of earthmoving and mining equipment, was having problems with Lincoln and vice versa. CAT was headquartered in Peoria, just over one hundred miles from Moline. Since Frank felt a change in personnel would help, I was offered the Peoria office in addition to Moline. My job was to heal the rift between the two companies.

Since I had been eyeing Chicago or some other larger city for a promotion, combining the Moline and Peoria offices was equivalent to a move to Chicago in both sales and pay. Shirley was happy–we'd made some terrific friends in Davenport (that we still have today) and she didn't want to move our family. Much to our surprise, we had both fallen in love with the Quad Cities.

Once I'd spoken with CAT, I realized I had a larger problem on my hands than just Peoria. The ill will had spread to the outlying plants in Joliet and Aurora, which fell under our Chicago office. I called Frank and informed him that I would need these locations to fall under my umbrella as well if I were to put together a consistent program. Frank agreed and I developed a fine relationship with the salesmen in our Chicago office.

Both CAT and Lincoln were old-fashioned companies, deeply entrenched in the way they thought things should be done. In other words, both were used to doing things their way and both were stubborn as hell.

CAT's specifications for welding consumables had recently been modified to include their own specification code number—in lieu of the American Welding Society code number everyone else used. CAT demanded that their new code number be printed on every single package of welding consumables they purchased. The new code was part of CAT's internal quality control program, and to their credit, CAT was fanatical about quality.

Unfortunately, CAT's quality assurance requirements conflicted with Lincoln's manufacturing process. As our products came off the manufacturing line, they were immediately palletized, glued together, and placed in inventory. From our standpoint, it was ridiculous to tear pallets apart to place the CAT code on each individual package—especially at no additional cost. As the gridlock escalated, I could literally see thousands and thousands of dollars flowing to our competition.

Then I had an idea.

Why not PREPRINT the CAT code on ALL our packages ALL the time? There was so much printing on the boxes already that the addition of a simple IE-332 or IE-67 couldn't possibly matter to other customers. This logic struck home, and to this day, I believe CAT's codes are stamped on all Lincoln packaging.

CAT loved the idea and gave me credit for moving the immovable. We made some other simple and subtle changes that pleased the quality control group. I was becoming a sort of hero with the welding quality control folks. After about six months under my umbrella, things at CAT began to calm down.

Although I had great success in many areas at CAT, I still hadn't been able to budge Cleveland on the subject of MIG welding, and

Lincoln was losing tons of business to the competition in the farm implement industry. Unfortunately for me, the Midwest seemed to be the only part of the country acutely affected by the influx of MIG. The rest of the United States was not experiencing the draught in business that we were. In addition, with management's belief that steel mills could produce MIG wire more economically than we could, Lincoln was naturally reluctant to enter into a business where the company felt it couldn't be competitive. The fact that the steel mills never really entered the business was beside the point.

Contrary to farm equipment, construction equipment requires a very different type of welding materials. The steel is much heavier and the welding process uses a tremendous amount of submerged arc, an area in which Lincoln excelled. Tractor cabs, however, were made of sheet metal and used a smaller-diameter wire, the perfect application for MIG, and CAT used it.

Although Lincoln still did not make the type of wire CAT used with the MIG process, CAT did buy a significant amount of 5/64" diameter and larger from us. In fact, due to our higher quality and consistency, the operators preferred Lincoln wire to other less expensive brands and became quite vocal anytime CAT suggested using another supplier for those applications.

Although Keystone Steel and Wire had a manufacturing plant in East Peoria near CAT and the president of Keystone lived next door to the quality control manager at CAT, the welders at CAT refused to use Keystone's less expensive wire. This fact alone should have helped shatter Lincoln's resistance to enter the MIG wire business, but so far it hadn't even made a dent.

Knowing J. F. Lincoln was scheduled to visit Peoria to pay a call to both CAT and LeTourneau headquarters, two of his favorite customers, I racked my brain for a way to convince him to consider the MIG process.

Then I had an idea.

I petitioned my newly acquired "friends" in the quality control division for a favor. Since I knew that JF was supremely customer-focused, I asked CAT to petition him to have Lincoln manufacture smaller-diameter wire (.035 and .045) to CAT's specifications. I was counting on JF's dedication to our customers to drag the company into the MIG business. The quality control engineers at CAT were only too happy to help me out.

When JF arrived, the CAT group performed beautifully. JF told them he would have an answer within a week. True to his word, he sent a very competitive quote and L-50 WAS BORN! I'm sure JF knew what I was up to, but since CAT had asked, he couldn't refuse.

Oddly enough, for many years after L-50 was introduced, I couldn't convince Lincoln engineering, management, and especially our president, William Irrgang, to openly admit to manufacturing a product for the gas-shielded process. Today, I believe the L-50 type products used with the MIG process are the number one product in dollar volume for Lincoln. Obviously, these products are now openly marketed for what they are.

To this day, I have no idea why they fought so hard to prevent the proper categorization for this product. I think perhaps Irrgang felt that as long as our salespeople did not have a gas-shielded alternative, they would sell Innershield more aggressively and successfully—sort of like Cortez burning his armada after landing in the Americas. I guess only my trip to Lincoln Electric heaven will unravel this mystery.

My territory exploded with the introduction of L-50. Right behind CAT was John Deere, who immediately approved the product. Deere had always preferred Lincoln and they were relieved that we had finally decided to wake up and smell the coffee. In fact, I think Lee Allgood actually beat me out for the first official production order for L-50 for John Deere, Des Moines. Other large accounts quickly followed suit. Sales skyrocketed and our team saved not only the Moline office but there's a good chance we saved the future of the entire company. Had Lincoln not introduced L-50 when they did, there's a good chance the entire company would have been left in the dust.

JF died shortly after the introduction of L-50. Little did I know that his vision would die along with him.

In addition to our consumables, the CAT Joliet Welding Engineering and Manufacturing Groups had always used Lincoln six-hundred-ampere motor generators as a semiautomatic welding power source. They had over one hundred of these machines in the fabricating area alone. However, a new team of players at CAT had recently emerged. Their first order of business was to begin replacing our generators with three-phase rectifier power sources in order to save power and reduce noise. Not a bad idea, really, except that Lincoln didn't manufacture three-phase rectifiers (not yet).

Once again I hit the wall that was William Irrgang. When JF died in 1965, Irrgang had taken over as CEO and chairman. Prior to his promotion, Irrgang had run engineering with an iron fist. He resisted change of any kind, especially in our product line. Now CEO, he still flat out refused to give the engineering department authorization to develop a design for a three-phase rectifier! I wasn't the only salesman asking that Lincoln develop this machine, and we were all tearing our hair out trying to understand Irrgang's reluctance to keep up with the competition. I really missed JF.

CAT liked Lincoln and wanted to stick with us as a machine supplier. They also liked Tom Farris (from the Chicago office) and me. Finally, when I approached Irrgang with a direct request from CAT, he reluctantly agreed to come up with a design. After about six weeks, we still had nothing from engineering. CAT, unaccustomed to being ignored, gave us an ultimatum: either produce a quote by 4:30 p.m. the following Friday afternoon or lose the business.

That fateful Friday, Tom and I made frantic calls to the Lincoln general sales department all afternoon from CAT Joliet. They were stymied. Irrgang, for some reason, did not "feel inclined" to set a price!

I nearly choked. As we watched the minutes tick by, Tom and I couldn't believe what was happening. This was *Caterpillar* for God's sake! The two of us just stared at each other, speechless.

Then a light went on.

At approximately 4:00 p.m., unable to wait another second and unwilling to give up a huge amount of potential business, Tom and I shot out the door into the CAT parking lot. We hauled Tom's portable typewriter out of his car and plopped it on the trunk of his Pontiac. After some quick calculations, we invented a price, typed the quote on Lincoln letterhead, and made a mad dash for the purchasing department. Tom and I handed the quote to CAT as the clock struck 4:30.

Lincoln received an order for six machines the following week. Fortunately for Tom and me, Frank Boucher honored our fictitious, albeit very competitive, price. Three phase rectifiers became a standard at Lincoln, and once again, CAT had led the way.

Looking back, I'm surprised Tom and I didn't get fired on the spot! Thank you, Frank. Looking farther back, I realize that my CAT quote wasn't the first time I'd pulled a stunt like that and taken matters into my own hands. Sometimes I wonder how I made it as far as I did. Taking risks can be a tricky business.

My first year at Harvard Business School I got homesick—for my parents, for my beloved California, and for Deborah, my longtime girlfriend from Pomona College (but not necessarily in that order). I desperately wanted to go home for Christmas, but I didn't have the money for a commercial flight.

Then I had an idea.

I still had my military police uniform from the 399th Military Police Battalion in Pasadena—well, most of it anyway. Although I was still technically part of the Reserve Battalion, since I was now in Boston, I was no longer an active participant.

Once classes let out for the holidays, I donned my uniform. I then persuaded a classmate to drive me to Westover Air Force base in Springfield, Massachusetts, where I hoped to catch a ride on a military transport.

Once he dumped me at the air base, the minutes turned to hours, the hours into days. My vacation was quickly disappearing. Sometime in the wee hours of the morning of my second day lurking around the air base, it suddenly occurred to me that I might be asked to produce papers in order to board the flight. Obviously, I had none.

Then I had another idea.

It had not escaped my notice that I was the only schmuck waiting around at that ridiculous hour. Mulling over the need for official documentation, I spied a typewriter at an empty desk. Sitting huddled in a corner, I typed up fictitious orders requiring me to report back to the 399th Military Police Battalion in Pasadena. I signed (well, forged, actually) my commander's name. To this day, I can't believe I did that.

After three long, tense, and disappointing days, a DC-3 finally arrived in Springfield from Iceland, headed to Riverside, California. I gathered my suitcase and walked nonchalantly onto the plane. Acting as if I had every right to be there, I quickly took a seat. Although my uniform was impeccable, technically I was out of regulation: I was wearing civilian shoes. Somewhere between Los Angeles and Boston, I had lost my military boots. I laid my suitcase across my feet and went to sleep.

Fortunately, no one asked to see my papers or noticed my missing boots during the flight. After a stop in Tulsa, Oklahoma, we landed in Riverside about 11:00 p.m. I assumed I was in the clear. However, to my horror, as we touched down, I spotted the military police waiting to meet the plane. Word had spread that some civilians had been caught boarding holiday flights and the MPs were checking for nonmilitary passengers.

Damn.

Then I had yet another idea.

I stood up and flashed my military police officer's insignia at the waiting MPs. I immediately volunteered to supervise an "orderly deplaning" of service personnel to proceed to inspection. While the MPs were busy with the first group of soldiers, sailors, and airmen, I grabbed my suitcase, strode purposefully in the opposite direction, hopped a low concrete wall, and headed for LA.

Although my dad was surprised and happy to see me, he did NOT approve. Not anxious to visit me in Leavenworth, he bought me a return ticket to Boston. For the twelve days I was home, every time he looked at me, my father just shook his head.

So much for being clever, Don.

(But it worked.)

-16-

3,276,640 Pounds
(If I spell that out,
it's almost a whole
paragraph!)

THE MOLINE AND Peoria offices didn't attract much attention from Cleveland—even with two of the company's largest customers smack-dab in the middle of the territory. It didn't help that there were no direct flights from Cleveland to either city. We were lucky to see anyone from the main plant more often than every two or three years.

So how does an ambitious young man lost in the cornfields of a neglected area attract the attention of his superiors?

He has ideas. And one very BIG idea.

I would simply set a record for the single largest order in Lincoln's history! *Sure, Don, no problem.* If I somehow managed to pull that one off, they would have to notice me.

Obviously, I went back to my friends at CAT. Since the problems between our two companies had been solved, Lincoln was enjoying a steady stream of orders from CAT for our welding consumables, the "razor blades" of our industry. I had secretly been keeping a close watch on the order dates and the volume of each order.

I decided to approach my friends in the purchasing departments of the Illinois plants with the following pitch: if CAT would agree to preorder their consumables ALL AT ONE TIME, Lincoln could really facilitate delivery. With CAT's orders up-front, Lincoln would be able to ensure excellent on-time delivery. I practiced my speech about fifty times before presenting the idea to CAT. I had only omitted one minor detail: Lincoln *already* had excellent on-time delivery. A *very* minor point in my book.

Fortunately, my buddies at CAT were happy to help me out. I don't know if they had any idea what I was really up to and I had no desire to find out. It sounded good.

In those days, orders were typed on special paper. To make my presentation even more dramatic, I used props. I bought a small toy Caterpillar tractor and a fake silver platter. I stacked the orders on the platter, wrapped them carefully with tissue paper, and placed the tractor on top. I then secured my "gift" in a box and mailed it to Frank Boucher in Cleveland.

Don Hastings, Lincoln District Manager of the often-overlooked Moline and Peoria offices, presented the vice president of sales with a stack of orders from Caterpillar Tractor totaling 3,276,640 pounds of consumables.

They noticed.

In fact, the entire production made such an impact that I received accolades from both Frank Boucher and William Irrgang. Frank referred to my stunt as "good histrionics," which it was, of course. Too bad JF hadn't been there. I think he would have gotten a kick out of it.

I spent a total of seven years traveling to CAT's headquarters in Peoria and to their various plants in East Peoria, Joliet, Aurora, and Decatur, Illinois, and I loved every minute of it. CAT became Lincoln's single largest customer and I believe they are still one of their largest customers today–if not THE largest.

I understand that Lincoln recently held a board of directors meeting at CAT Aurora. Board members were offered a tour of the facilities and CAT showcased Lincoln products at every opportunity. It's fun to think I just may have had a little something to do with that.

In 1970, I received another call from Frank Boucher asking me to meet him at Chicago O'Hare International Airport. During lunch, he asked me to consider moving to Cleveland to become General Sales Manager. The position required extensive travel as I would manage thirty-five district offices throughout the United States. He seemed hesitant. He counseled me to consider the position carefully and talk things over with Shirley.

The hesitation in Frank's voice was uncharacteristic of the man sitting in front of me–almost as if he were unsure of offering me the position. Before he could recant, I blurted out, "I'll do it."

Frank was shocked.

I didn't care. I wasn't about to give him time to change his mind.

-17-

The Rust Belt

IN 1970, THE country was hit hard by a recession. Knowing that the moment I hit Cleveland I would be consumed by my new job, Shirley and I escaped to Florida for a few days. I met up with Jack Roscoe, who was now in Miami. Over lunch, I got an earful of what was in store for me in Ohio.

Jack had gotten tangled up in some type of corporate politics and Al Patnik, Jack's assistant in Cleveland, had stepped in. Because Al was in good favor with the Lincoln family, in lieu of being fired, Jack had been offered the district manager's position in Miami, a huge step down. Good old American *know-who* at its finest.

Al pulled all the strings he could to get Jack placed in Miami. Due to his connections with the Lincoln family, Al believed he would be offered the general sales manager position after Frank. Fortunately for me, he was wrong.

Jack, of course, owed Al. When Al realized he was not going to be the next general sales manager, as he and many others had thought, he asked Jack to return the favor. Al wanted to report directly to Frank, then vice president of sales, bypassing me altogether, yet still working in the general sales office. Jack pulled a few strings of his own, and this strange setup awaited me in Cleveland. Jack was kind enough to warn me of my pending drama. I guess Al, who was considerably older than I, just couldn't stomach reporting to a forty-one-year-old. I appreciated the heads-up, but this was turning into a soap opera.

But there was more. Much more.

Jack also informed me that Frank was suffering from cancer and was keeping it very, very quiet—thus the reason for bringing me to Cleveland. Since Frank had held two positions, both vice president of sales and general sales manager, the Powers That Be had decided to split Frank's job and give the General Sales portion to me. Frank retained his title of Vice President of Sales.

The ugly truth is that once William Irrgang found out Frank was ill, he had forced Frank to find his own successor ASAP. To expedite the process, both Irrgang and Frank wrote a name down on a piece of paper and simultaneously revealed them to each other. My name turned up twice.

I finally understood Frank's hesitation to offer me the job. The whole process must have been horrible for him. Less than two years later, he died of cancer and I was given the rest of his job and his title as Vice President of Sales.

Under the circumstances, it didn't feel like a promotion.

-18-

Unions: Boom to Bust

T HE LINCOLN ELECTRIC Company World Headquarters is located in Euclid, Ohio, an eastern suburb of Cleveland. When Shirley and I arrived in 1970, although a recession was looming, the area surrounding the plant buzzed with heavy industrial activity. Now only Lincoln remains. The area is destitute.

What caused the demise of all these businesses? One word: unions.

In the early 1900s, many manufacturing companies considered their human labor to be a necessary evil. Except for a few visionary companies, labor practices bordered on the barbaric. Workers were pushed to greater and greater output, under atrocious working conditions, without commensurate pay. Enter: unions. They rose as the "protectors" of the workers and the right to strike was a very effective weapon in the war between management and labor. Unions gained incredible strength during the 1940s and 1950s.

As negotiations progressed over the years, a new middle class was born. The unions became stronger and stronger, successfully utilizing both real and potential strikes to wrest control from management during contract negotiations. To avoid devastating strikes, countless corporations simply caved in to union demands. Many tried to raise prices to cover the additional labor costs but were unable to sell their products at the increased prices. Consequently, both sales and profits took a huge hit.

Neither side of the conflict recognized competition looming from enlightened management abroad who happened to have the added advantage of lower labor rates. Sales dropped further. Profits declined. Trouble brewed whenever a contract came up for renewal. The problems were not insular to Cleveland. Detroit and numerous other Rust Belt cities became desperate.

The following is a list of industrial companies near Lincoln that were thriving when I arrived in Cleveland but have since either gone out of business or moved their manufacturing operations to friendlier environments—namely those without union hostility:

Addressograph Multigraph

Euclid Road Machinery

Fisher Body Division of General Motors

Chase Brass and Copper

TRW

Parker-Hannifin

Eaton Corporation

This abbreviated list includes only those companies that were based in Euclid—and it represents merely the tip of the iceberg. A compilation of all Northeast Ohio companies who were forced to close their doors would be too depressing to mention.

Although both Parker-Hannifin and Eaton Corp. still maintain their headquarters in the area, they have both moved most of their manufacturing facilities to right-to-work states. The two companies are prospering today.

The irony of this situation is that unions, originally designed to protect workers, have, in reality, eventually hurt the very people they were anointed to protect. Outrageous demands forced companies to close or relocate, eliminating the very jobs the unions had been consecrated to ensure.

Prior to my arrival in Cleveland, the UAW had poked around Lincoln from time to time over the years. However, they were never able to secure a foothold inside the company. For the most part, Lincoln employees simply weren't interested. *They were making too much money.*

In those days, there was only one employee entrance to the Lincoln Electric parking lot. To enter our property, employees were forced to drive past crowds of picketers at one or another of the neighboring companies. We watched as one company after another was crushed by labor demands. The neighborhood took on a ghoulish air as once-thriving businesses crumbled, busy parking lots turned into deserted concrete slabs, and rusted fences with locked gates stood like skeletons against the grey Cleveland sky. After the carnage, the only detectable life in those haunted lots belonged to the occasional weed that poked its head through a black, twisted crack in the cement—and the occasional rat.

As an aside, in 1962, President John F. Kennedy signed Executive Order 10988, paving the way for public sector unions. Although I am a fan of JFK because he dragged my uncle, Patrick McMahon, to shore (with the strap of Patrick's life preserver between his teeth) in the PT109 episode during WWII, I believe public sector unions were initiated for purely political reasons as a way to finance the reelection of their preferred politicians. Obviously, they were not there to protest adverse working conditions (as the private sector unions had been), and I believe the public sector unions and the politicians they've paid for have done more to damage our cities that any other single force.

Of course, that's just my opinion.

As an additional aside, my uncle Patrick was the dark horse in the family. Although he was lucky enough be rescued by a future President of the United States (who subsequently appointed him Postmaster General of San Diego), as a teenager Patrick hadn't been smart enough NOT to get caught frolicking around in a haystack with my grandmother, Patrick's stepmother. By the time the PT109 incident occurred, Patrick had been shunned by the family for quite some time.

-19-

No Room at the Inn

EVEN THOUGH I knew about the strange setup that awaited me in Cleveland, I was eager to start my new job as General Sales Manager. There were only two problems: there was another movers' strike on (so we had no furniture once again) and the general sales office had not prepared for my arrival.

To put a roof over our heads, the Lincoln family stepped in and came to our rescue. Jim and Emma Lincoln and Marjorie and Harry Carlson offered us a vacant cottage owned by the Lincoln family in their compound in Mentor-on-the-Lake, a community on the shores of Lake Erie. Their offer was a godsend and prevented Shirley from turning around and driving the girls back to Davenport. Homeless and pregnant is one thing; homeless with three kids is something entirely different. I think that cottage saved my marriage.

When I arrived at the general sales office, I didn't have a place to sit. Since my job was actually a spinoff of Frank Boucher's responsibilities and my presence made Frank all too aware of his illness, management hadn't made any provisions for my arrival. I think maybe Frank was hoping it was all a bad dream. Fortunately, Bob Dalzell, the motor sales director, was out on medical leave, so they ushered me into his office. It didn't even have a door on it. To add insult to injury, Frank had to share his executive assistant with me.

Needless to say, my first few days were more than awkward. I spent my first six weeks sitting in Bob's area. Even more bizarre, after JF died, Irrgang had never moved into JF's former office. It was as if the space were being preserved as some kind of shrine to JF. I knew Irrgang revered JF, but this was ridiculous.

Once Bob Dalzell came back, it was going to be chaos. Irrgang finally made the move to JF's office, Frank moved into Irrgang's office, and I moved into Frank's old office. I guess it took that long for them to decide to let me stay.

Al Patnik was also waiting for me in his new nebulous role as I'm-not-exactly-sure-what. Since Al reported directly to Frank Boucher, then later Irrgang, I always felt a little like Al was spying on me. Since he didn't report to me and I wasn't privy to his job description, I didn't know what to do either with him or about him. Al reminded me more of a hovercraft or spy satellite than part of my team, so more often than not, I simply ignored him. I didn't care for this setup one bit, but those were the cards I'd been dealt. Since I couldn't beat the system, I forced myself to work within it. What a stupid situation.

To top off this overwhelmingly warm reception, apparently Frank had also "forgotten" to give me a raise. I had been so excited about my promotion to General Sales Manager that I'd never brought up my compensation package. I'd just assumed I would be given a salary increase commensurate with my new position and the Greater Cleveland area. I was wrong.

Maybe Frank really did forget (which I have a hard time believing) or maybe he subconsciously believed that if he didn't pay me, I would go away. Either way, it was a mess. I never said anything and Frank never did either (living through the Depression really bit me on the backside on that one). I didn't get a raise until Frank died two years later. With the cost of living significantly higher in Cleveland than Davenport, another movers' strike, and all the traveling I was doing, Shirley just *loved* my new job.

The one bright spot in this miserable setup was that Frank's executive assistant finally got fed up with her dual role and *strongly suggested* I hire Marylee Baller, a clerk in the general sales office, as my executive assistant.

I did.

God smiled on me that day.

Marylee was smart, dedicated and a key to my success. She stayed with me until I retired, and I wouldn't have reached the top without her. She became part of our family, and my daughters used to kid me that I could fall off the face of the earth, and as long as Marylee was still at her desk, no one would notice.

I know I should write more about Marylee. She was a huge part of my business life, my family's personal life, and an integral factor in my success for nearly twenty-seven years. How do I describe a woman who was not so much an executive assistant but more an efficient, calm, and steady presence that permeated everything?

-20-

Smoke

WILLIAM IRRGANG WAS intimidating. He was a force. Throughout my entire career I referred to him both publicly and privately as "Mr. Irrgang" or just "Irrgang." In fact, all these years later, I still think of him that way. I can't explain why I never referred to him by his first name (nor did anyone else, come to think of it), but if you'd ever met him, you'd know.

Irrgang was German by birth, an electrical engineer by education, and a highly intelligent man. He had immigrated to the United States following the hyperinflation in Germany during the 1920s, was subsequently hired by JF, and was CEO when I arrived in Cleveland as General Sales Manager. He was also completely inflexible and stubborn as a rock.

Irrgang was "JF's man," and while CEO, he defended JF's product lines and policies as if JF were still alive, which was part of the problem. JF died in 1965 (with his boots on) at the age of eighty-five, but unfortunately, his visionary leadership died with him—at least as far as Irrgang was concerned.

Irrgang was a brilliant engineer. He came up through the company in the manufacturing division at a time when many Lincoln products practically sold themselves. (Lincoln had completely "sold out" all products during WWII.) He believed that if something isn't broken, don't fix it—or improve upon it in anyway, lest the upgrade disrupt the manufacturing process.

However, now was a time when the industry was rapidly changing and we were not. Our competitors were developing new products at an alarming rate. As Vice President of Sales, I could not persuade Mr. Irrgang to direct our talented design and manufacturing engineers to jump into the market opportunities that were staring us in the face. In fact, the doors to the engineering department were kept *locked* during business hours—engineers locked *in*, everyone else (particularly the sales department) locked *out*. For someone full of ideas to move the company forward, this setup defied all rational thought.

I learned later that Lincoln was simply doing what they'd always done—make the products they wanted to make, regardless of market demands. As a salesman trying to please the customer, this philosophy drove me crazy.

Then one night, about 5:30 p.m., as I was finishing up some paperwork, I smelled smoke. Since Irrgang and I were the only two people still working in the executive offices, and his office was next to mine, the smoke could only be coming from there. I knocked on his door.

Wow.

Sitting before me was a completely different man from the one I had argued with only an hour before. Sixty minutes prior, he and I had hit an impasse over the paint color for the welding machines for our consumer and light industrial products. Now, Mr. Irrgang was leaning back in his chair with one foot on his desk, completely relaxed. In a rare show of courtesy, he asked me to come in and sit down. As he seldom asked anyone to take a seat, I usually found myself standing in front of his desk like a peasant before a medieval lord. He liked to maintain a position of power and authority to keep the rest of us off balance.

It worked.

That evening, I noticed that Irrgang was twiddling a half-smoked cigar between his fingers. Until that moment, I had never seen him smoke anything but cigarettes. At that time, we had a strict ban on smoking until after 5:00 p.m. in both the factory and the office. He must have recently found a taste for cigars. An ex-smoker myself, I had seen tobacco soothe the savage beast, but never to this magnitude.

Hmmm.

Then I had an idea.

I brought up our paint problems once again. Instead of brushing me off as he had only an hour prior, pontificating that it was a manufacturing issue and not a sales issue, he graciously suggested I meet with Neal Manross, the vice president of manufacturing, to take another look at it.

I couldn't believe it. I had witnessed a miracle.

Obviously, when Manross heard that Irrgang was open to modifications in the color and finish of the machines, he was more than cooperative—a nice change. Neal had chosen the paint himself, a horrid rust color and, unless specifically instructed from the top, had no intention of changing it. We chose a bright Lincoln red—to the accolades of employees and customers alike. Later it was pointed out to me that that Neal Manross was color-blind.

From that point on, whenever Irrgang was being particularly obstinate about an important modification to a policy or product design, I would wait to approach him until I smelled smoke. I estimated the time it took him to smoke about half a cigar, then I quietly knocked on his door. Within the Hastings clan, this system became known as the *cigar tactic* and I used it to my advantage on numerous occasions.

One of my biggest "cigar victories" was the evening I finally persuaded Irrgang to officially recognize our L-50 welding wire (designed for CAT) as an official American Welding Society gas-shielded product. Up to this point, due to his resistance to gas-shielded processes in general, he had insisted that L-50 wire be coded only as EM13K, the code for submerged arc welding. His stubborn refusal to recategorize the product was hurting sales.

Although the metallurgical tolerances were basically the same for both gas-shielded and submerged arc welding, many customers would only buy products carrying the AWS code for the gas-shielded process. Although L-50 had been designed for the MIG process for CAT, it didn't state that on the box or in our literature. About three-fourths of the way into his cigar, he finally agreed to change the code to AWS ER70S-3, the official code for gas-shielded welding.

Whew!

Such a simple change, but internally at Lincoln, the relabeling was a tremendous open admission that we had entered the gas-shielded arc welding arena. To ensure future success, I bought an elegant humidor in Chicago, filled it with fifty ridiculously expensive Cuban cigars (don't ask), and presented it to Irrgang. I didn't want him to return to just smoking cigarettes. Ever.

Shortly after the L-50 recategorization, we came out with a new cored wire that we called *Outershield*, the name a tongue-in-cheek spoof on our very popular *Innershield*. I had a brilliant advertising campaign all ready to go. I wanted to photograph Irrgang sitting in a large wing-backed chair, smoking a cigar, wearing an Ohio State sweater with the big red *O* on the chest. The caption underneath would read, "OUTERSHIELD. 'You never thought I'd do it.' –signed *William Irrgang*." I just knew the ad campaign would be a hit, but no amount of cigars would budge him. I lost that one–not the product, just the ad.

Although the cigar tactic was effective, it wasn't always immediately successful. It took me five years, the last two filled with cigar smoke, to convince Irrgang to allow engineering to redesign the Weldanpower (behind locked doors, of course). Once Irrgang's smoke finally cleared, our engineers came up with a winner in no time flat. I think they'd had the design stashed in a drawer for years.

They didn't teach this tactic at Pomona or Harvard.

Perhaps they should.

-21-

Manufacturing Minus Sales Equals Scrap

DURING MY TIME as General Sales Manager (which was only two years until Frank died) and subsequently as Vice President of Sales, I was on the road constantly–or more accurately, up in the air. With thirty-five district offices, plus the independent agents, Big Three in Texas, Lincoln Big Three in Louisiana and Alaska, and 117 technical presentations to various American Welding Society sections all across the country, my daughters were raised in a matriarchy.

Since Lincoln did not own a private jet, I logged more than my fair share of frequent flyer miles. At one point, United Airlines informed me that I had been invited into their inner circle as a member of their Million-Mile Club. I'm not quite sure what that says about me as a husband and father, but I was having an awfully good time.

The most important thing I ever did while I was General Sales Manager and Vice President of Sales was to develop our sales force. Due to economic downturns and an overwhelmingly engineering- and manufacturing-dominated mentality, by the time I was promoted to

General Sales Manager, there were huge gaps in the Lincoln sales ranks. The left-brain side of the company was always a little suspicious of us right-brained salespeople. We were considered to be, at best, a "necessary expense."

Prior to my arrival, Lincoln had imposed a hiring freeze in the sales department, and we had no new hires coming up through the company. Since it had always been my motto that *manufacturing minus sales equals scrap*, I knew we would soon be facing disaster. A recession was on the horizon and salespeople generate revenue, period. If we were to survive the coming upheaval, we couldn't continue to leave large territories unattended.

The heavens must have heard my pleas—the hiring freeze was soon lifted. I immediately began recruiting new people. Because Lincoln has a highly technical product line, sales are most often application-driven. Consequently, we required our salespeople to be degreed engineers and we trained the hell out of them. I'm not sure when that policy was officially instated, but I suspect I got in just under the wire.

I have always looked to hire people that I believed would relate to our customer base. No matter how highly trained technically, if your sales force can't communicate or establish rapport with your customers, they are doomed. It wasn't always easy to find the right candidates. In a pool of qualified engineers, I looked for anyone who had played sports and/or had some talent outside their chosen field of engineering. Success is most often a cooperative effort, and sports-oriented individuals understand team efforts. Among the athletes, I even managed to find a couple of classical pianists! I ended up with a very diverse and talented group.

My first hire was Dick Seif, an engineer and MBA from Michigan State. He fit my profile perfectly. Dick became a stalwart in the sales department for roughly forty years. He became president and CEO of Lincoln Canada and later vice president of sales and marketing of Lincoln North America. His keen mind and quick wit always kept me on my toes. Still do, as a matter of fact. He is the genius behind the title of this book.

Next, I grabbed John Stropki, who had worked summers at Lincoln while getting his engineering degree from Purdue. John was smart, tough, and did a terrific job. He shot up through the organization to become chairman and CEO of Lincoln and has just recently retired.

I then hired S. Peter "Pete" Ullman, a Cornell engineer and captain of Cornell's gymnastic team. Pete became part of the family. He and I went to war on the tennis court, and we were known to continue our play well after dark—*in* the dark. We played "by ear." Because Pete was in superb condition, rather than run myself ragged, I played with his mind and emotions. Occasionally, especially as he was about to serve, I even went so far as to grab my heart and feign chest pains. More often than not, he double-faulted. The fact that he never begrudged me my victory was a smart career move. Pete eventually became CEO of Harris Calorific.

Doug Bull, a Lincoln legacy and engineer out of Tulane University, also became a bona fide member of the family on an airplane at thirty-thousand feet. A group of Lincoln guys and I were on our way to a meeting in Reno, and my daughter Jane, along for the subsequent weekend ski trip, was too young to be admitted to the shows in the casinos.

Then I had an idea.

I bought Jane and Doug fake wedding rings at the airport and they pretended to be newlyweds on the plane. They put on such a good show that half the passengers bought them drinks. I consoled myself with the knowledge that if my daughter were breaking the law, at least she was doing it "married" to a Tulane engineer and classical pianist. Since I had orchestrated the entire charade, I couldn't say a word. Jane and Doug talk about their "honeymoon" to this day.

In addition, somewhere along the way I was also fortunate enough to recruit Chris Bailey and Mike Mintun. Chris has led the robotic automation division to unprecedented heights, and Mike has assumed my former position as vice president of sales and marketing. I can't wait to see where they go from here.

Over the years, I went on to hire the most unbelievable groups of young men I have ever had the pleasure to meet. In the fifteen years I led the sales department, they continued to surprise me with their ingenuity, depth of talent, and supreme dedication.

I also shied away from those I didn't feel would make the appropriate impression. I remember meeting one highly qualified young Cornell engineer for breakfast. He ordered eggs, sunny-side up, bacon, and toast. At the end of the interview, his plate was clean. There was just one problem: he'd never picked up a fork! He'd lapped up his eggs with the bacon and toast.

I didn't hire him, though I never told him why. Looking back, I should have said something. I often wonder what he's doing today (and if he ever learned to eat with silverware).

Outside the traditional Lincoln training, I brought these guys into my private life. Shirley and I made them members of the family—in fact so much so that Shirl often had to kick them out of the house. We entertained them in our home, played tennis together, and went on ski trips as a group. We became friends, held together by respect and a common purpose. And we laughed. We laughed at the company, we laughed at the stress, and we laughed at each other. And out of all this silliness came brilliance on multiple levels. I can't stress enough the value of inviting people into your life. I often asked myself, *how could work be this much fun?* Fun, hell. It was exhilarating!

I was always preaching to my guys to be *i*maginative, *c*reative, and *i*nnovative:

I-C-I. I'm sure they got sick of my spiel. I wanted them to think outside the box. I hoped that my creative solutions and programs would not only give them great ideas to work with but also give them permission to use their own imaginations.

They did. They consistently surpassed my wildest expectations.

Then I had an idea.

To further fire up my guys, I scheduled a series of regional sales meetings. I charged the troops to exhibit I-C-I at the meetings and challenged them to come up with something unique.

I held my first meeting in Los Angeles. Toward the end of the day, the guys put on a hilarious skit focused around various sales situations entitled "How the West Was Won." It was brilliant.

I landed in Cleveland gushing praise for the West Coast offices. Via my enthusiasm, I was daring others to take up the challenge. Wow. I don't know if it was jet lag or the pressure of the job, but I completely underestimated their competitive natures.

My next meeting was in Boston and the offices went all out, adding terrific energy and atmosphere to the meeting. As these gatherings continued across the country, word spread like wildfire and each office tried to outdo the others. My tour culminated with the regional meeting in Cleveland. At that time, the Cleveland region had the oldest and most tenured sales force. They were known to be the stuffiest and most conservative bunch in the company. I couldn't wait to see what would happen.

As 1980 was an Olympic year, the Cleveland region named their meeting the LincOlympics, spearheaded by Pete Ullman. The meeting was a day-long skit centered on the company, various sales scenarios, and me. All the participants dressed in elaborate costumes. Much to my chagrin, I was elected to preside over the festivities and they demanded that I don the appropriate attire—as Caesar, no less, in full Roman regalia (toga (a bedsheet), laurel wreath (don't ask), and flip-flops tied with string).

I was amazed to see the grizzled old veterans shed their numerous years and tight constraints to join the younger ranks in a spirit of unbridled fun. I know that the energy and creativity that went into those meetings spawned an identical phenomenon *in the field*—and was a key ingredient in the success of our recession-busting programs.

Looking back, I'm not sure how many novel business ideas came from the sales force underneath me, but their imagination, creativity, and innovation knew no bounds when it came to spoofing either me or the Lincoln Electric Company, and they poured this same energy and enthusiasm into implementing my ideas. They put on skits at sales meetings that had everyone in hysterics. These guys were incredible and there was no greater group on the planet when it came to execution. I still marvel at the enthusiasm and dedication they showed on a daily basis.

People are willing to fight to the death for their friends, and if you run a company, you can have no better friends than a loyal and dedicated sales force. On more than one occasion, one of my daughters would catch me staring at the group and mumbling, "I just *love* these guys!" I'm sure they felt that. I couldn't believe what a superior group of people I had the privilege to lead. I literally couldn't wait to get to work every day.

-22-

Stinkin' Lincoln

AT THE SAME time I was building the sales force, I traveled throughout the United States meeting our distributors nationwide. I attended my first NWSA (National Welding Supply Association) annual meeting in San Francisco in 1975. I came to understand that on a national level, our company was thought of as *Stinkin'* Lincoln.

I'm just guessing, but this dubious distinction could have had something to do with our low dealer margins, lack of marketing support, and propensity to neglect them in general. In those days, it wasn't unheard of for dealers to march into my office, pound on my desk, and demand my attention, with a few choice words thrown in for good measure. I couldn't blame them.

In fact, the distributors were suffering from an identity crisis of sorts. Lincoln tended to call them *dealers,* JF had referred to them as *middlemen*, and they preferred to be called *distributors*. Needless to say, everyone was confused and Lincoln's relationship with these companies had suffered because of it. For the purpose of this book, I've used the two terms interchangeably, reflecting the confusion we all felt at that time. Call it poetic license.

Although I had developed terrific relationships with my dealers as a salesman in Northern California, apparently I was an anomaly. Since we sold to them at reduced margins, the company as a whole thought of distributors as a necessary expense. I set out to change that particular Lincoln philosophy. From now on we would treat the distributors as *valued customers,* which they were. With JF gone, it wasn't an easy sell.

Throughout my tenure as Vice President of Sales, I made myself highly visible on the NWSA circuit. From regional meetings where I was the featured speaker, to six zone meetings every spring, to the national meetings, I kept showing up, asking questions and listening, listening, listening. I asked one question over and over: "How are we doing? How are we doing?"

Through those years, the answer I received was "better and better all the time."

In his speech to GAWDA (Gases and Welding Distributors Association, formerly NWSA) in Las Vegas in 2009, Jack Butler from Butler Gases in Pittsburgh presented me with an award and stated the following:

"At many of the early meetings in the 1980s, I'm sure Don wore a flak jacket as he took verbal bullets from many independent distributors and company stores. Back in the early 1980s, MIG was a four-letter word at Lincoln Electric, but not with Don Hastings. Don was changing Lincoln from *Stinkin'* Lincoln to a prodistributor, proprofit and, of course, pro–end user manufacturing company. The gray machines at a 10 percent gross margin and red machines at 20 percent were beginning to become more profitable and the margins began to slowly but surely improve.

"I think Don saw many NWSA distributors as new potential salespeople for the growing Lincoln force. Don even brought a marketing side to the old direct sales manufacturing company. Don was initiating change with Lincoln, and he kept working the NWSA meetings with his constant 'How are we doing? How are we doing? How are we doing?' ... Don set an elevated bar for new manufacturers in our industry. Don became one of us ... a trusted friend and ally of the NWSA."

I really did try to make these guys my friends and I think I did. I participated in everything I could. I played tennis and golf and skied with them. I even went to a couple of Pittsburgh Steelers games with Jack (although I did root for the Cleveland Browns, of course). Lincoln's relationship with our distributors improved immensely. Little did I know how important these relationships would become when the company hovered on the brink of disaster.

-23-

Stand Up

IN ADDITION TO flying to our district offices and dealer meetings, I was also a member of the Steel Plate Fabricator's Association (SPFA), which met at various resorts around the country.

In the mid 1970s, on my way to a week-long SPFA meeting at the Broadmoor Hotel in Colorado, I noticed that my suitcase was heavier than usual. Heaving it out of my trunk at Cleveland Hopkins Airport, I felt something pop. My lower back. I limped into the terminal, determined to continue my trip.

During my layover at O'Hare Airport in Chicago, I happened to run into a friend from the Quad Cities who just happened to be a physician. I explained my ailment in great detail, and he was kind enough to write me a prescription on the spot. It read, "Let's have a drink."

OK.

Over the next year and half, the pain became more and more acute. I could no longer sit down. Since my girls were still in school, Shirl was unavailable for taxi service. Consequently, I had to ask Bob Dalzell to drive me to and from the factory. This is not so strange in and of itself until you realize that we had to switch automobiles so Bob could drive Shirley's station wagon with yours truly lying down in the back.

When I reached the office, I had to stand up all day. My back felt as if it were on fire, with red-hot daggers poking me every time I moved. I did allow myself a few short breaks, holding meetings while lying on my back on a lunch table in our cafeteria, a sight that became all too common as the months dragged on. I used a chest-high set of bookshelves in my office as a stand-up desk.

Unlike me, Bob liked to leave the office shortly after 5:00 p.m. I, on the other hand, routinely scheduled special meetings with the trainees or visiting salespeople until 6:00 p.m. or later every evening. However, since Bob was driving, we left when he wanted to. My after-hours contingent simply followed me home. My daughters nicknamed me the Pied Piper.

Upon my arrival, I enlisted Shirley and whichever of my three daughters happened be handy to act as hostesses. Shirley was constantly scrounging around in the kitchen for enough food to feed the unannounced straggle of trainees or stray salespeople. I was in traction on the couch and my daughters chided me for "holding court" each evening.

Around 11:00 p.m., Shirley, finally having had way too much fun for the last few hours, began playing with the lights. She would switch them on and off as a not so subtle hint that it was time for the troops to return to their own tents. For such smart guys, they could be a little thick. It often took up to an hour to get them out the door.

Mohammed couldn't go to the mountain, so the mountain came to Mohammed, or more accurately, Mohammed's living room. This stupid setup went along for almost eighteen months.

Finally, one night after the troops had finally left, the pain was so severe that I couldn't get off the couch. Rather than attempting to stand, I rolled myself onto our coffee table, fashioned from an old ship's hatch cover. I thought maybe I could use my arms to push myself off. Nope. I couldn't get off that either. In fact, I could barely breathe. In that one moment, I cried uncle and decided to let the surgeon cut.

My orthopedic surgeon, Les Nash, told me later, "In my twenty years in the operating room, you are the only patient I've ever operated on that I knew would feel better in the recovery room than you did going into surgery." He was right. I hadn't simply slipped or ruptured a disc; I had shattered one. The disc had broken into seven pieces, and each fragment had lodged itself somewhere up my spinal column. Had I known how bad it was, perhaps I would have succumbed to the knife sooner, but I doubt it. I was deathly afraid I would end up paralyzed. Back then, spinal surgery was a little iffy (at least to me) and I have the zipper to prove it.

Thank you, Les, for making sure I can still walk (constantly), ski (occasionally), play tennis (sporadically), and pretend to play golf.

-24-

Leopards

THE RECESSION OF the early 1980s hit Lincoln hard, sparked by skyrocketing inflation and sharply higher energy costs. Over an eighteen-month period, our domestic sales, which had been steady and strong, plunged nearly 40 percent. Even with factory hours reduced from over fifty hours per week to thirty and thirty-two, we still had more employees than necessary. In our executive meetings we contemplated enforcing the doctrine that employees had to have two years of service before guaranteed employment kicked in.

Although we could have enforced that rule and laid off the most recent hires, the new people were talented, well educated, energetic, and valuable additions to our workforce. I really felt it would be ethically wrong to let them go, not to mention very bad business—especially at Lincoln. Our internal morale couldn't take it.

I lay awake at night trying to figure out a way to save our employees while simultaneously salvaging our dying bottom line. The executive committee was really pushing to reduce the workforce, an option that made me shudder. Obviously, since I was the loudest proponent of holding on to people, it was up to me to figure out a way to make that happen. I had the hat; now I just needed the rabbit.

Then I had an idea.

Lincoln had just developed a new machine, the SP-200, specially designed for gas-shielded auto body and light sheet metal welding. Although it functioned beautifully, it was kind of a big, bulky thing, considering its application. True to form, Irrgang hadn't allowed engineering to design a new case—he had insisted they use an existing design. (To everybody's relief, it was later redesigned in a much smaller box and renamed the SP-100.)

As the SP-200 was new to the market, I wanted to make a splash. But before we launched it, I needed a guinea pig to field-test the machine. Unfortunately, the economy was so bad that I couldn't afford to spare any of our sales force. I looked around for an alternative.

Then I had another idea.

My daughter Leslie had graduated early from Stanford University in Palo Alto, California. Since the formal cap and gown ceremony was still three months away, Leslie wanted to backpack around Europe (or some such nonsense). I thought it would be much more fun for her to stay in Northern California peddling welding machines up and down the Pacific coast. What well-bred young lady wouldn't jump at the chance?

Fortunately, Leslie had attended welding school at age sixteen (another of my brilliant ideas), so she was no stranger to sparks. She did inform me that she drew the line at wearing dresses and pantyhose (my suggestion): one, they would melt; two, she would melt. It was well over one hundred degrees in Northern California that spring.

I can't remember why she agreed to forgo her trip to Europe to do my bidding, but I'm sure it involved some kind of bribe on my part. Or guilt, perhaps. Or maybe I told her it would look great on her résumé. I can't be certain.

Whatever the reason, she swallowed my pitch and soon after we set Leslie up with a demonstration truck and two full days of training. For the next three months, Leslie made sales calls up and down the San Francisco peninsula field testing the new machine. She reported to David Fulton in the general sales department. At the end of her adventures, Leslie wrote up a report detailing the pros and cons of the machine, the setup, and the sales pitch. We saved what worked and threw out what didn't–including Leslie. She wasn't exactly upset about that.

Both David and Leslie did an outstanding job. The program was ready for blastoff. There was only one problem: I was shorthanded.

The SP-200 had been designed for small shops, new territory for Lincoln direct. Due to the economic catastrophe surrounding us, my guys were concentrating on trying to dig up all the business they could find from larger fabricators. They didn't have time to address the smaller specialty markets. However, I really wanted the new machine to make a splash in the marketplace, and I still needed a sales force to work with our distributors. Where would they come from?

Hmmmmmm.

And then I had another idea. A crazy idea.

What if we offered both factory and office hourly workers an opportunity to volunteer to become sales assistants in our district offices? With the drastic reduction in our sales volume, the factory personnel were currently underutilized. Why not move them to where they were needed? Given the choice between sales and unemployment, I was sure we would get a good response. Well, pretty sure.

Irrgang signed off on the program one evening, cigar in hand. In 1981, the Leopard Program was born.

Since it wouldn't work to force people to move into sales (sales is difficult enough for people who *want* to sell!), I had to define the opportunity clearly and hope for the best. The response was overwhelming! We selected fifty-four factory and fourteen clerical workers out of a pool of over one hundred active volunteers. After a few weeks of special training on the SP-200, the Leopards were sent into the field from Maine to California. Essentially, the Leopards were looking for "spots" of business not previously covered by Lincoln. They worked primarily with our distributors.

We called the program Operation Leopard, and the sixty-eight new sales assistants were nicknamed Leopards as they were out "prowling" for business. They had definitely "changed their spots," both literally and figuratively. A simple title, I admit, perhaps even a little corny, but highly effective.

During the next two years, the Leopards brought in about $2.8 million in new business from a market Lincoln had previously left untapped. It also gave our distributors a whole new list of customers. Because it was such a unique program, the Leopards got a lot of press not only around the industry but throughout the entire country—which helped both their attitudes and our bottom line.

Although I had always believed that the program not only saved jobs but paid for itself, today I'm not so sure. It did, however, show our hourly workers that management was dedicated to guaranteed employment even beyond the board-approved two-year service commitment.

We didn't lay <u>anybody</u> off. I'm really proud of that.

Once sales started to pick up, we called the Leopards back to the plant. Several of them never returned. They stayed in the field, mentored by their district managers. Many pursued further education, took a sales position with another company, or changed careers. I can't say I was sorry to hear that. Some had already earned master's degrees and one even had a PhD. A former Leopard is now a Lincoln regional manager. I was and continue to be extremely proud of them all.

Due to the severity of the economic downturn and the easy solution layoffs could provide management in general, I realized that if faced with a similar situation, not many future executives would be willing to stand behind guaranteed employment, especially if they had not come up through Lincoln as I had. In an effort to keep the program alive, I asked the board of directors to change the guaranteed employment policy. Although I didn't like doing it, I recommended they offer the program only to employees with three or more years of service rather than two. They readily agreed. After what I had just been through, I was sure future management would appreciate this modification.

Today, David Fulton is President and CEO of Hartland & Company, a $13-billion investment counseling firm in Cleveland. Leslie is a writer. In fact, you're reading her work.

As an aside, later, when we finally redesigned the SP-200 to make the smaller, more compact SP-100, I made a bet with the factory superintendent. I bet him that I could sell the new machines faster that he could produce them. I had no idea he would throw massive effort into winning that bet. Needless to say, I lost.

I must admit, I loved the competition and the spunk displayed by the people in the shop. To reward the plant personnel for their efforts, I posed for pictures pretending to carve a big black bird and wearing an apron that said, "Eating Crow and Loving It."

The guys in the shop kidded me about that bet for years. It was worth it.

-25-

Damned Dealers

THE LEOPARDS WERE off and running. However, there was no way they would be able to offset the downturn enough to keep the plant busy. I needed a way to generate sales in larger volumes. We had been working tirelessly with our current distributors, but their sales had fallen off as well.

Then I had an idea.

Why not sign up more distributors?

Hmmm.

I knew that each new distributor would be contracted for an initial order of forty thousand pounds of electrode (one truckload) and at least six machines. If we could sign up enough new dealers in a short period of time, we would be able to generate enough volume to keep the factory busy. Even though sales to distributors weren't as profitable as selling direct, we could make up the dollar difference in pure volume.

Volume makes money. Just call heaven and ask Sam Walton (no, the *other* heaven).

Low sales are a morale killer, and I knew I had to get the sales department fired up. To get everyone energized, we put together a short adaptation of the movie *Patton*, highlighting the most dramatic aspects of the story. After three days of editing, we had it cut down to sixteen minutes—and we were off to the races.

I called a special meeting for all the district managers. In an uncharacteristic move, instead of holding the meeting at the plant, I held it at the Marriott Hotel in downtown Cleveland. Since I was promoting a program that would seriously compete with our existing distributors, I couldn't risk being censored by upper management. I'll admit my approach was a little sneaky, but I didn't need an uninvited, hostile audience raining on my parade.

Despite my clandestine efforts, Ted Willis, our president, caught wind of what I was up to and snuck into the meeting. After the sixteen-minute *Patton* film and my presentation of the 100 Days' War, Ted was on board. I shouldn't have been surprised—Ted had been an army major in WWII and was fiercely protective of the production side of the business. More volume meant saving jobs.

We dubbed the program the 100 Days' War because we wanted a major impact to our bottom line in roughly three months. Our managers loved the idea. I held six regional meetings around the country with mandatory attendance for our technical representatives. They hit the ground running.

At the end of three months, my guys had signed up two hundred thirty-two new major distributors across America and I had managed to single-handedly "piss off" a good portion of the four hundred we already had. I was lucky they didn't drop Lincoln, but they sure weren't bashful about letting me know exactly what they thought of my new program. Obviously, word had hit the street that the buck stopped with me.

At a minimum of forty-thousand pounds of electrode and six machines per dealer, the 100 Days' War produced orders for over nine million pounds of consumables and almost one thousand four hundred machines. Ted was happy. Irrgang didn't object.

Over the years, I spent a great deal of my time courting our distributors. Through various programs and ample personal attention, I somehow managed to regain the trust of our original group and turn them into a formidable sales force for Lincoln in their own right.

In 1997, I was honored at the National Welding Supply Association's (NWSA) Annual Meeting in Philadelphia and again in 2009 by the Gases and Welding Distributors Association (GAWDA–formerly NWSA) in Las Vegas for contributing to the tremendous growth of welding supply distributors. Little did they know that my dealer program was born out of my own desperate will to survive.

Pomona Victory troop ship: My home for two weeks
(along with two thousand other green troops straight out of basic
training) heading for Japan as part of the occupational forces following
WWII. This ship and my dad's suggestion that I check out Pomona College
(in Claremont, California) caused my life to take
a sharp turn for the better. (1946)

Commanding colonel pinning the Medal of Commendation
on twenty-year-old Donald Hastings for becoming the
number 1 cadet in the Eleven Western States ROTC Summer
Training Camp, Fort Lewis, Washington. (1949)

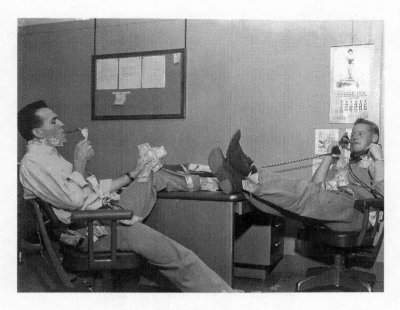

A young, brash Don Hastings (left) with Chet Shira (right)
as sales trainees, celebrating our first bonus. (1953)
Courtesy of The Lincoln Electric Company, Cleveland, Ohio, USA.

William Irrgang (left) receiving the famous Caterpillar orders from Frank
Boucher (right) for 3,276,640 pounds of welding consumables. (1965)
Courtesy of The Lincoln Electric Company, Cleveland, Ohio, USA.

Yours truly "eating crow" after losing a
challenge to the shop workers. (1973)
Courtesy of The Lincoln Electric Company, Cleveland, Ohio, USA.

Bonding with some of my guys while skiing in Park
City, Utah. Left to right: Lou Kleinsmith, Doug Bull,
Don Hastings, Dick Seif, and Jerry Siko. (1976)

With Marylee Baller, my executive assistant for
twenty-seven years, Cleveland, Ohio. (1987)
Courtesy of The Lincoln Electric Company, Cleveland, Ohio, USA.

Shirley Diane Tedder Hastings—trophy wife for sixty years.

With Shirl when I received the AWS Counselors Award for outstanding service to the welding industry. (2001)

Donald F. Hastings, CEO and Chairman of the Board, the Lincoln Electric Company, Cleveland, Ohio. (1995) Courtesy of The Lincoln Electric Company, Cleveland, Ohio, USA.

-26-

Mind over Matter

WHILE TED WILLIS was CEO, there was plenty of competition within the company for the presidency. I was up against other qualified individuals, including some family members, and we were all interviewed by the nominating committee of the board of directors. Lincoln defined itself as a manufacturing company, and since I had moved up through the sales department, I was more than a little suspect. With the exception of a brief stint in sales by JF when he first joined his brother, JC, no one had risen to the top of the organization through the sales department in the history of the company. In my pursuit of the presidency, I was bucking a strong current.

Then I had an idea.

In preparation for the grilling by the nominating committee I knew I would receive, I tried to foresee possible questions they would ask so I wouldn't be taken off guard. The evening before my interview, I rehearsed my questions and answers with Leslie. I knew that the major question would be "If you were not a candidate, Don, who would you recommend as the best choice for president?"

I had Leslie ask me that question over and over until I could quickly and easily reply, "Go outside." I truly didn't believe there were any internal candidates that I could endorse—other than me, of course. The interview happened exactly as we had practiced.

While I was Vice President of Sales, I was introduced to a new concept, Silva Mind Control (now it's called the Silva Method of Meditation, for obvious reasons). The program in Cleveland was presented by Friar Justin of the Franciscan Hermitage in Indianapolis. The hermitage describes itself as an "international, interfaith life center dedicated to the spiritual, physical, intellectual, and professional growth and formations of persons of all persuasions and circumstances."

Having been raised by a mother who was a devout Christian Scientist, I was well aware of the belief in the power of the mind, especially in relation to physical healing. Due to my mother's beliefs, my sister (Betty), brother (Bob), and I were all born at home. It's hard to imagine today. We never went to the doctor as kids and I didn't receive my fist vaccination until I was seventeen, when the US Army vaccinated me for smallpox.

I had personally seen the power of the mind/ belief work miracles. In fact, in my second year at Harvard Business School, I had somehow managed to spontaneously heal myself of a broken neck.

During my second glorious autumn at Harvard, we challenged Tuck Business School from Dartmouth to a touch football game. Since everyone had played varsity football in college, the blocking was fierce. In fact, our star player, Dick Kazmier, was a Heisman Trophy winner from Princeton. I was playing defensive end. I ran headlong into a blocker, pushing me backward, while simultaneously suffering a hit from behind. In the crunch, I heard something snap.

I lay motionless on the field until someone finally realized I was really hurt. One of the players called an ambulance and I was rushed to Massachusetts General Hospital. After a series of x-rays, the doctors confirmed that I had cracked my C5 vertebra. The doctor called my parents. Speaking to my mother, I overheard one of the doctors say, "We think he'll live."

Live? Who said anything about *not living?*

Although my mother remained in Los Angeles, she and I both prayed fervently for my healing. And then I prayed some more.

Two days after I was admitted to the hospital (and the doctors had decided I would actually make it), they ordered another series of x-rays. The staff needed precise pictures in order to fit me with a neck brace. As the technician was taking pictures, I noticed he became more and more agitated. At one point, he left the room. He returned some time later with the orthopedic surgeon, and the two of them must have x-rayed my neck twenty times looking for the break. Where did it go?

I can't explain what transpired during those two days, but I do know that a cracked vertebra is rarely "here today and gone tomorrow." From their stern looks, I got the feeling that the medical community considered it extremely "bad form" on my part to just go and heal my own neck like that. Now–you–see–it, now–you–don't is a cruel game to play on the medical establishment.

A couple of days later, I was fitted with my leather brace and told to wear it for six months or until I could easily turn my head. Although there was no sign of the fracture anywhere in the x-rays, I was not in a hurry to tempt fate. I wore the brace for six months, eliciting the proper amount of sympathy from coeds in the Greater Boston area. (Hey, use what you have.)

It should come as no surprise that the combination of my Christian Science background and the miraculous healing of my C5 vertebra left me open to concepts many others felt were a little, uh, shall we say, *on the fringe*. Consequently, the Silva material was right up my alley.

The eighteen-hour Silva course was a real eye-opener. A couple of the guys in the general sales department joined me in the training. In essence, Friar Justin taught us to meditate in order to achieve a self-hypnotic state of mind. We then visualized different scenarios, controlling our breathing, thoughts, and emotions. Beyond that, we were taught that while we were in a hypnotic state, we could influence *others*.

Friar Justin taught Silva in the original format and I can remember him saying, "This program is powerful stuff and is *not* to be used for anything negative. You not only have the power to influence your own life, but you also have the power to influence the thoughts and actions of others."

Wow.

I was so impressed with the concept that I encouraged our entire sales force to attend the training sessions in their area and give it a whirl–Lincoln would pay half. A number of them did.

Given my Silva training, in my pursuit of the presidency, I figured it couldn't hurt to try to influence each board member's opinion of me in a positive way. I visualized each person sitting in the board room. While in a meditative state, I mentally said to each one of them, "Don Hastings is the best choice for president. He is intelligent, has a strong work ethic, knows the market, understands our product line, is well respected in the industry, is trusted by our employees, and wants the position. Give Don the job."

I have no idea how much effect my mental gymnastics had on their decision, if any, but I got the job. I could hear my high school sweetheart Carolyn's (you remember, the blonde) mother (also a Christian Scientist) telling me as I drove her around Beverly Hills and Bel Air in my 1940 Mercury convertible (the one that got me in trouble), "Look at these beautiful homes, Donald. You can have a house like these if you work hard and believe you can have it. Believe in yourself, Donald, see it happening and one day it will be yours."

Carolyn's mother and my mother had a lot in common–other than me, of course. I had learned from the best.

-27-

Hail to the Chief

(JFK was right. It *does*

have a nice ring to it.)

I N 1987, WILLIAM Irrgang died. George E. "Ted" Willis became CEO and I became President and Chief Operating Officer (COO) of Lincoln Electric North America. (I got a bigger office immediately this time.)

At that time, Lincoln had no mandatory retirement. Irrgang was in his late eighties and still CEO and chairman of the board when he died, as was JF when he passed away at eighty-five. Ted Willis was sixty-eight when he took over the reins. The reason our CEOs had a tendency to die in the saddle is that they had waited so long to get the job in the first place. Once they finally reached the top, they didn't want to step down. I can't say that I blamed them. I had my eye on the top spot, but with Ted becoming CEO at the tender age of sixty-eight, it looked like I might have to wait forever.

By the time I was promoted to President, Lincoln was back on track. Other than my responsibility for the sales department, as General

Sales Manager and Vice President of Sales, I oversaw the Maintenance department. I think I was given jurisdiction over maintenance as a test to see if I would screw up. Since there was an inherent mistrust of anyone who had been in sales, giving me responsibilities outside of my supposed comfort zone had been a setup. I wasn't the only one who wanted the job of president and I believe certain players were rooting for my failure. I think they may have forgotten that I had gone to business school. I ran the Maintenance department without a hitch.

I moved easily into my new job. After all, I'd had my eye on the presidency ever since I joined the company.

-28-

MBWA: Management
By Walking Around

EVER SINCE JF died, I'd had the feeling that something was missing from upper management. As a company, we had so much pent up energy and enthusiasm in so many different areas that I knew we could do more. I missed JF's dynamic, visionary leadership.

As CEO, Irrgang, in an attempt to remain loyal to JF, had refused to let the company move forward with new products. He stuck to the NIH (Not Invented Here) syndrome. If we didn't develop a product or process from start to finish, we wouldn't manufacture it. Consequently, the welding industry had blasted right by us in a number of specific markets.

When I took over as President, I vowed to change that. It was time to take off the gloves and enter the fight. Ever since my days in the Moline office, I had been dragging the company kicking and screaming into the future. I needed a way to pry its claws out of the past.

Fortunately, I had an idea.

JF had walked the factory floor each day after lunch. Following in his footsteps, I bought a pair of steel-toed shoes and headed for the main shop at our World Headquarters in Euclid. If Lincoln were to move forward rapidly, I knew I needed to recruit the employees in the plant to the new thinking. If we were going to expand our product line at a rapid pace, incorporating higher technology, I needed to get to know the people in the factory and make sure they were on my side.

When I hit the floor, I was immediately taken aback. It appeared that Irrgang's staunch determination to remain stagnant had somehow trickled down into the shop. My first day in the factory, I met a man who performed his job on one of the assembly lines with his shins wrapped in newspaper secured with duct tape. When I asked him why he came to work gift-wrapped, he replied that he kept banging into a piece of metal that stuck out from the line. He told me that he had mentioned the problem to his supervisor, but nothing had ever been done about it. Padding his bruised shins with the *Cleveland Plain Dealer* was the best solution he could come up with. I had the metal piece cut off immediately. He lit up like a Christmas tree.

Shortly thereafter, I came across a woman working in a dimly lit section of the factory. She performed close work and was squinting over her station. I noticed that there was nothing but a single low-wattage lightbulb high above her head. When I asked her if she would like additional light, I thought she was going to cry. We installed a higher-wattage lightbulb and gave her a lamp. So simple.

In addition to solving a myriad of minor problems, my MBWA gave me a chance to talk to the people in the factory. I knew this generation had higher expectations than those of their predecessors. I also knew that a satisfied workforce meant less supervision, higher quality, and as a result, greater profits. It's no secret that people who take pride in their work build a better product. I made it my mission to get the factory workers more involved in the overall manufacturing process, thus instilling more pride in their accomplishments and making them, well, happier.

Then another idea popped into my head.

I began meeting with each assembly station in the factory and asking the workers what management needed to do to make their work easier, more reliable, and more repeatable. The first couple of times

I asked these questions, I saw jaws drop. I don't think anyone in the factory had ever been approached by management outside the shop, especially the president. I didn't need to say much after that. Once they realized I was on their side, the dam burst and ideas flowed.

To make sure management didn't drop the ball on follow through, I appointed a special quality committee, in addition to our advisory board, made up entirely of factory personnel. They met weekly with the shop superintendent and monthly with me. We listened to a myriad of small issues and simply made it a priority to take care of them one by one. Enthusiasm jumped.

My objective was to tie quality to job satisfaction. I truly believe that people take great pride in building things of value. My goal was to build quality into every step of the manufacturing process rather than just test for it at the end of the line.

Looking back, I think I was subconsciously attempting to change the company's culture on the factory floor. I wanted the employees to *want* to build in quality for personal reasons, not simply to do it because they knew mistakes would be caught by inspectors at the test stations. In addition, no employee wanted to have to correct his/her mistakes—especially on personal time, a policy that still exists today. I wanted our employees to feel that each machine that came off the line was like a building block in the foundation of a cathedral. I know that sounds corny, but I really thought of it like that.

Within a short time, we were able to cut the number of line inspectors by 25 percent and the number of employee-caused errors by 50 percent. I was so impressed by what our workforce had accomplished that I pushed upper management to invest in a multimillion-dollar powder paint system that would apply an automotive quality finish to our welding machines and motors. Willis thought I was crazy, but with the new paint system, we not only *built* the finest machines in the world, but they finally *looked like it*.

In a 1989 *Industry Week* article, I stated the following: "We want to build the best in the world. Even though we are a very productive company and have been the price leader for a long time, if we don't have the best product in every aspect—from design to manufacture to packaging to shipping—we will have a front row seat to our own destruction. That's what happened to Detroit." I still believe that.

I loved every minute of my time on the factory floor. Once our people realized that I was not looking to find fault in any way but rather dedicated to finding areas where I could assist them, the entire endeavor became a wonderful experience and one that I treasure today. If I were to give advice to almost anyone in a manufacturing organization, it would be this: *Walk the factory floor and get to know your people.* You will be amazed at what you find.

Once the plant was on my side, we stepped up R&D and began adding new products. Plans were in the works to expand our product line to include plasma cutting, oxy-fuel cutting, and MIG guns and cables as well as expanding our hard-facing alloys. We added plants in Brazil, Mexico, and Japan. We went so far as to have the Japanese plant blessed in a Shinto ceremony.

It was also during this time that Ted Willis, our CEO, set his sights on Europe. ESAB, a Swedish company, had been buying up manufacturing facilities in the United States. I think Ted considered ESAB's action an invasion of the United States, at worst, and incredibly bad manners, at best. As a veteran of WWII, he had a natural distaste for anything resembling encroachment on America.

Ted immediately sprang into action and went "shopping" in Europe. By purchasing foreign companies, Ted planned to be strategically prepared to take advantage of a unified common market come 1992. He wanted a strong Lincoln presence overseas. He planned his strategy with our outside legal counsel—who also happened to be a Lincoln board member at that time. I would often spot them in Ted's office huddled over their notes.

To complement this new aggressive stance, the company also had to become more adept at hiring. Traditionally, Lincoln promoted from within. As technology rapidly advanced, we were losing out on the new breed of technically savvy graduates. We began recruiting the best and the brightest from the universities.

My first foray into the new high-tech recruiting world netted me four Harvard MBAs. Although also a Harvard Business School graduate, I was happy to find guys who had finally decided it might be smart to make *things* rather than *deals.* I don't think the stock market crash of 1987 hurt my recruiting efforts.

Much to their chagrin, I immediately put the MBAs to work on the assembly lines. I needed the people in the plant to know these guys weren't just hotshots–they were real people who were willing to do the tough jobs. I'm not sure the MBAs appreciated my ground-floor approach, but it worked.

The company also started a new program to finance advanced education for our employees. I knew that if we were to stay ahead of our competition, our people would need to be smarter.

Speaking of smarter, Shirley came to my rescue in 1987. Shortly after I became President, Lincoln purchased a manufacturing operation in Mexico City. About a year later, they were to pay their first small bonuses and I was invited to say a few words to the employees. I wrote my speech in English, of course, and was promptly informed that the speech would need to be given in Spanish.

Fortunately, we had a trainee from Mexico in our welding school. He was kind enough to translate the speech into Spanish that would be acceptable to the Mexico City audience. Since I had taken two years of Spanish in high school, I began rehearsing at home.

On about my fourth run-through, Shirl cried out, "Donald, I can't stand it. Your accent is so bad they won't understand a word you are saying!"

I replied, "OK, smarty-pants, why don't you give the speech?"

She did. Unable to bear the thought of our audience cringing as I butchered their language, she bravely stepped up to the plate. A Southern California girl born and bred, Shirl had taken six years of Spanish, one of those years at a college level at Pomona. Her accent was perfect.

Shirl hit a home run. She received a standing ovation from an audience of over two hundred Mexican workers. We couldn't wait to show the video to our friends, family, and the Lincoln group. Unfortunately, the video photographer had forgotten to turn on the camera.

¡Dios mio!

-29-

Affirmative Action in Action

IN THE 1980s, affirmative action was in full swing, with an emphasis on hiring African Americans. In an effort to comply with the regulations, we gave tremendous effort toward hiring African American employees. This was quite a challenge since at that time, Euclid, Ohio, was primarily inhabited by people of Eastern European descent. People like to work where they live, or at least fairly close by. At that time, we just didn't have many people of African American descent in the environs surrounding Lincoln. That has since changed.

Fortunately, we were able to find a number of qualified workers. As time went on and the new employees realized we would treat them fairly, they began recruiting their friends.

One fine day, the State of Ohio Affirmative Action Committee marched into Lincoln unannounced. We welcomed them to tour our offices and factory, expecting to receive their blessing without incident. They had other ideas.

"You're in violation of our equal opportunity laws."

What? How was that *possible?*

"You don't have enough women on the factory floor."

Oh.

Women? Who'd said anything about women?

Good God!

Lincoln is a manufacturing facility. Many of the jobs in the factory require a great deal of upper body strength as the parts and finished products are heavy and cumbersome. Where, exactly, were we supposed to put these women?

"Unless you correct this situation by the time we return in three months, you'll be fined by the state."

Wow. Ouch.

We immediately formed a women's committee of three senior female factory workers. Within sixty days, we had hired the proper number of (athletic) young women. However, this caused more problems that it solved for us internally.

Because we pay people so well, many of our factory workers spend their entire careers at Lincoln. Consequently, young new hires are often given the more physically demanding jobs. As workers gain seniority (i.e., get older), they are moved into less strenuous positions. Since there were some jobs the women just weren't physically capable of performing, we had too many people for too few positions. Internal battles ensued. I began to understand how many old guard military must feel about the influx of women requesting combat. How does one be fair yet realistic while remaining diplomatic and politically correct while trying to run a profitable business (or a war) at the same time?

We finally figured it out, but the solution was a more painful process than we had expected. As part of the integration, we ended up offering a voluntary early retirement program for a few of our most senior workers.

After that, we were able to let natural attrition take its course. I'm happy to report some of those women are still at Lincoln today.

As an aside, there is a place for diversity in the workplace, but when it is based on quotas rather than on hiring and retaining the most qualified people to do the job, it hurts not only the company but the country as a whole. Lincoln's success was built on hiring people who were motivated to improve themselves and their families. We were very fortunate to find women who had the same motivations—and who could easily lift at least 50 pounds.

-30-

Game Changer

ONE AFTERNOON, I was discussing Republic Steel with the sales representative who covered the account. He was telling me of his troubles, namely that even though he was offering the customer a cost savings, he was getting nowhere.

"What should I do?" he asked.

Hmmm.

In welding, as in other manufacturing processes, there are many ways to perform various tasks. The choices in welding machines are critical but few. More important is the choice of consumables: electrodes, flux, and wire. There are hundreds of sizes and types to choose from to achieve maximum quality and lowest cost for any particular application. This is where highly trained technical sales representatives can really shine.

We needed something to catch Republic Steel's attention. They seemed perfectly happy with a competitor's product even though it was higher cost.

Then I had an idea.

"Why don't you *guarantee* the cost savings to the customer?" I asked him.

Stunned, he replied, "Can I do that?"

"You bet, but *over my signature*." And voila! The Lincoln Electric Guaranteed Cost Reduction (GCR) program was launched.

Lincoln technical representatives are trained to find cost reductions. In fact, they each have to present a cost reduction somewhere in the company to pass training. This program was even stronger. We had never guaranteed it before—well, almost never.

Actually, I have to admit that at some point in my career I had gotten wind that Lincoln had previously implemented a guaranteed cost reduction program of some sort in the past. However, the program had been discontinued prior to my arrival. With a few modifications and a modern approach, we put together a very effective program.

Lincoln technical reps approached potential customers with a simple request: "Let me survey your shop floor. I will demonstrate alternate methods to lower your costs. Lincoln will give you written documentation of the reduced costs, plus a letter from our president promising that if our new idea doesn't actually achieve our stated result, we will give you a cash settlement for the difference."

Who would turn *that* down?

The GCR program was simple yet powerful. I had to send out a few checks, but it was an excellent investment. Sales climbed. We made the GCR a symbol of courage within the sales force even when we had to send a check. It took real brass to guarantee a savings to a customer when you knew the president of the company was guaranteeing your work. Tech reps were actually awarded one or two extra bonus points just for valor. We later expanded the program throughout Europe.

It was a real game changer.

-31-

60 Minutes

(There *is* no catch.)

Y OU KNOW YOU'RE having a bad day when *60 Minutes* knocks on your door.

In 1992, during my presidency, the *60 Minutes* television show contacted us. The show wanted to do a documentary about Lincoln's successful yet controversial management system. At that time, *60 Minutes* had a reputation for exposing trouble wherever they could find it. I think they still do.

I mentioned the interview to my colleagues at NEMA (National Electrical Manufacturers Association) and they thought I was crazy to even consider it.

They had one thing to say, "RUN!"

I welcomed them with open arms.

Lesley Stahl was the journalist assigned to us. She spent three days interviewing factory workers, office employees, engineers, management, and me as President. At that time, *60 Minutes* interviews were known to be extremely probing. Translation: The show was digging for dirt to embarrass their intended target as their approach created juicy stories. People tuned in just to watch their next victim squirm.

As the camera crew descended upon us, we were all nervous. I began to seriously question my decision to let them in. What had I been thinking? By that time it was too late; they were already inside the plant. Many of our people thought I was nuts. I have to admit, at that moment, I was inclined to agree with them.

After three days of shooting film, Lesley marched into my office, plopped herself in a chair, and announced that she was bored. She informed me that Lincoln was an average company and wouldn't make much of a TV story. I looked at her and sighed.

Lesley then asked me, *oh, so casually*, if she could sit in on an advisory board meeting "just to see for myself." Although she looked and sounded like a perfectly composed human being, I couldn't shake the feeling that deep down she probably had more in common with a lioness circling in for the kill.

The agenda for the advisory board meeting was designed as a platform to allow employees the opportunity to verbalize problems, lodge complaints, and present new and creative ideas. I realized she was hoping the advisory board was our Achilles's heel and she would hit pay dirt.

Oh, hell. Why not?

The meeting had been in session for about fifteen minutes when Lesley made her entrance. As usual, the twenty-seven advisory board members were addressing various aspects of their jobs—and mine. In general, they wanted improvements in working conditions, overtime policy, monitoring of supervisory transgressions, and even small requests, such as an additional drinking fountain on the factory floor.

Lesley Stahl or no Lesley Stahl, it was critical that I listen carefully to what the members brought up. I couldn't afford to miss anything that could become a major issue later on. One fact was obvious: this group was not there to praise the president.

I introduced Lesley to the group. Before I could say another word, she announced, "I haven't found anything worthwhile about your company. At this point I feel it has been a waste of time and effort. I'm bored!" Of course, by "worthwhile," she meant sneaky, suspicious, or clandestine.

And therefore, newsworthy.

Silence.

I held my breath.

The room exploded in a cacophony of excited voices. As if attacked from behind, the advisory board turned on Lesley Stahl! I couldn't believe it. Instead of bashing management (per usual), they actually praised the company! One member after another told her that Lincoln was a great organization and explained how lucky they were to work there. They even stated that management was open and honest with them, praising Lincoln's open-door policy. I actually received accolades for personally listening to them! It reminded me of certain family dynamics: *"We* can criticize each other all we want but *you'd* better not say a word."

Lesley was shocked! Clearly, she thought she was about to unearth the Lincoln skeletons. Curiously, although she had not found the dirt she was hoping for, she had at last found the hot button for her story: *A workplace employees actually praise?* Lesley was sounding less like a reporter and more like an unwilling character in an episode of *The Twilight Zone.*

Lesley continued her interview with a completely different attitude and the enthusiasm in the room became contagious on both sides. By *60 Minutes* standards, I had witnessed a miracle!

When the program finally aired some months later, no one had any idea how *60 Minutes* would portray Lincoln. Needless to say, I was more than a little apprehensive. If anyone could take lemonade and turn it back into lemons, it was the crew from *60 Minutes.*

Much to our shock, when the show aired, it made a really positive statement about Lincoln. They praised our values, our open-door policy, our incentive system, our guaranteed employment, and our overall concern for our employees. I believe it was the first noncritical episode of *60 Minutes* in history—and maybe the last.

The interview ended with Lesley asking me, "With all the positives about Lincoln, what's the catch?"

I answered simply, "There *is* no catch. There's no catch at all."

When the TV segment was over, I let out a huge sigh. I suddenly realized I'd been holding my breath for the past twenty minutes.

-32-

The Gathering Storm

THROUGH MOST OF my presidency, things seemed to be progressing smoothly. In 1991, I was elected Chairman of the Board of Governors of the National Electrical Manufacturers Association (NEMA) in Washington, DC. Lincoln was on the move in North America and the company was functioning like a well-oiled machine.

Admittedly, with all these changes during my time as President and Chief Operating Officer, some of our employees started asking questions. With their bonuses dependent on our cash position at the end of each year, they seriously questioned management, especially when it came to buying companies overseas. They were concerned that we may have been moving too fast, investing overseas too rapidly, and that their personal bottom lines may be adversely affected by the vast flow of dollars across the pond. I must admit, I had the same trepidations.

For more than a year before becoming CEO, I had been witnessing a troubling pattern. The individual European businesses would submit extremely optimistic sales and profits targets in their budgets. Unfortunately, they invariably missed the targets—often by quite a bit—and the gaps were getting wider and wider.

Even more worrisome, nobody seemed to have a handle on why the targets were being missed or what to do about the gaps. When asked, the managing directors would say, "We were too optimistic. The recession is worse than we thought. We'll downsize the budget." There was absolutely no fire in their bellies to correct the problem of declining sales.

In April 1991, a Lincoln board member (a very important board member, I might add) leaked to me that the top job would be mine at the end of July 1992. I've often wondered if he would have leaked that information had he not spotted me chatting with two of our competitors at the AWS Convention in Chicago.

My unease about Europe was getting serious. I took two short trips to Europe in late 1991 and early 1992. I was aghast at the managing directors' lack of concern about the need to boost revenues. They seemed perfectly content to just ride out the recession. I couldn't believe it.

Understandably, given Lincoln's history, the board looked at the situation primarily from a manufacturing standpoint. All four of my predecessors as Lincoln's chairmen had possessed engineering and manufacturing backgrounds and all four had held the firm belief that if Lincoln maintained the lowest cost, highest quality manufacturing operation, the company would automatically dominate the market—even though they were continuing to manufacture products the customer didn't want anymore. (How's that for logic?)

With my background in sales and marketing, I knew that high-quality, low-cost manufacturing would not be enough. Having a stellar manufacturing operation and a great product is a wonderful advantage, but if you don't have proper distribution, competitive delivery times, positive relationships in the marketplace, and people who can understand and help customers, you won't succeed. Period.

While he was CEO, James F. Lincoln had written that no company should ever grow larger than one man could administer or manage effectively (obviously, he wasn't *always* right). To our credit, we had exceeded that size even before we began the foreign expansion. We were already pushing the limits of the management skills and approaches that had served us so well when we were a smaller, simpler company.

When it became clear that we were primarily focused on improving the worldwide manufacturing operations by increasing efficiency and reducing costs, I decided to take my concerns to the board's nominating committee. I asked that the succession be accelerated and that I be given responsibility for Europe. I would use my sales and marketing expertise to increase revenues. "We should make a change," I said, but the committee said, "No, you've got to wait until next year." (That's the polite version of that conversation). I couldn't seem to get them to understand the gravity of the situation.

Although we knew that the foreign operations were in trouble, we continued to be outwardly optimistic. The board was confident that Lincoln's manufacturing prowess would enable us to make a success of the foreign operations.

As it turned out, the employees had been right to be concerned.

-33-

Sex Sells

WHILE ALL THIS nonsense was going on in Europe, I was still responsible for North America. I was always looking for ways to jump-start sales in new areas. From my early sales days in Northern California, I had come to appreciate motors. Although motors were not a great percentage of our overall sales and profits, they still represented an area where Lincoln could excel further. With our new paint system, the motors looked sharp.

I also knew from my experience in the Midwest that, from a competitive standpoint, a motor is a motor is a motor. The National Electrical Manufacturers Association (NEMA) developed minute and detailed specifications. Once a manufacturer complied with these specs, there was very little a company could do to distinguish one motor from another, making it virtually impossible to obtain a competitive edge from a technological standpoint.

Lincoln did have a unique stator windings protective cover, Multiguard, which provided the same or better protection to the windings at a lower cost than totally enclosed motors, but it was not enough of a competitive edge to grab a significant share of the motor business.

So, guess what? I had an idea.

People buy from people, especially where standardized products are concerned. As the father of three daughters, I thought, "Who better to market our motors than a bevy of beautiful women?" *A bevy of highly educated and well-trained beautiful women,* that's who (*and* the State of Ohio would certainly approve).

We hired fifteen sharp young women, including my youngest daughter, Nancy. All were college graduates and about half of them were graduate engineers. We trained them for several months, sent them out to our district offices, and assigned them motor accounts.

In addition, we instituted a five-year unconditional warranty, unheard of in the industry. We stepped up our advertising program and even offered free shipping.

Our Motor Ladies, as we called them, would become the talk of the town. At least that's what I had planned. Who wouldn't want to be called on by an attractive young woman with superior technical knowledge in an industrial marketplace? I was thrilled with our group. Motor sales and profits were on the rise and we were on the move. Or so I thought.

Now that the program was in place, all I needed to do was gather my guys together to fire up the troops.

-34-

The Top Job

WHEN TED WILLIS announced his retirement as chairman and CEO, I was President and Chief Operating Officer of North America. Although I was in line for Ted's job, nothing was certain. Since I was the only candidate to rise up through the sales department, I was again suspect. The board of directors all believed in Ted's comment to Harvard Business School:

We are not a research company.

We are not a marketing company.

We are a manufacturing company,

And we are the best manufacturing company in the world.

My only real competition for the top spot came from inside the Lincoln family. I hoped my enthusiasm, leadership, and performance history would prove thicker than family blood.

Even though I was witnessing some serious international problems developing and, to date, had been unable to inject my sales ideas into the international expansion, I really wanted the job. After much deliberation, the board finally elected me Chairman and CEO in 1992. I was sixty-three, just a kid by Lincoln standards.

I am truly fortunate that Ted decided to retire at seventy-two, the first CEO to do so voluntarily. Shirley remembers Ted's wife, Rolande, saying, "He is NOT leaving Lincoln feet first." As Ted has just recently passed away, had he not decided to step down, I would still be vying for the job—at eighty-five!

By the time I finally took over, I was chomping at the bit.

Ignorance is bliss.

I began this book with an excerpt from an article I wrote for the *Harvard Business Review* after I retired. The article began,

> At 5:01 p.m. on the last Friday of July 1992, I took over as Chairman and CEO of the Lincoln Electric Company. I had worked at Lincoln for thirty-eight years and had reached the pinnacle of my career.
>
> *My exhilaration lasted exactly twenty-four minutes.*
>
> At 5:25 p.m., while I was engaged in celebratory small talk in the hallway, our chief financial officer marched up to me and announced, "I've got some grim news. The numbers just came in from the European operations-- and they're bad. Very bad. They lost almost $7.5 million in June, and that means we'll have to report a second-quarter loss. We'll violate our covenants with the banks and default on our loans."

Needless to say, the motor meeting never happened.

Like I said, ignorance is bliss.

-35-

From Pink Cloud to Mushroom Cloud

DRIVING HOME HOURS later, I agonized over what I had just learned. The profits from our main operations in the United States wouldn't be enough to offset our losses abroad. And while Europe was our biggest problem, we also were losing money in Latin America and Japan. We would have to report a consolidated loss of $12 million for the quarter. In the ninety-seven-year history of the company, we had never experienced a consolidated loss.

Welcome to the top job, Don.

With the onset of the recession in 1992, the European operations deteriorated rapidly. The numbers reported in May and June were not good–the profits were marginal–and then came the awful news in July. The magnitude of the second-quarter loss caught everyone by surprise. Although I'd been openly worried, I had never imagined that the losses would be big enough to throw the entire company into the red!

Uh-oh. The bonus.

Despite a soft economy, our operations in the United States had done well. Our three thousand US workers would expect to receive, as a group, more than $50 million. If we were in default, we might not be able to pay them. But if we didn't pay the bonus, the whole company might unravel.

-36-

OK, Now What?

MY FIRST WEEK as CEO, I confirmed the magnitude of the crisis. I spoke with our managers in Europe and our international people at home. When I asked the Europeans whether they might be able to turn around their businesses quickly, they were pessimistic—the third quarter in Europe is traditionally the weakest due to shutdowns for vacations and holidays. They expected even poorer results.

In addition, there was no indication that our problems in Latin America and Japan were going to diminish. Our financial situation was clearly going to get a lot worse. Although I hated what I was hearing, at least they were honest with me.

Or so I thought.

In October 1991, I sent our New England regional manager overseas to teach the Europeans sales and marketing techniques that were highly successful in the United States, but he was rebuffed by his European counterparts. Apparently they were offended. It became all too clear that it would take CEO status, on-site, to catch their attention. I suddenly understood why the US makes little or no headway with foreign heads of state when we send our Vice President or Secretary of State to negotiate. Egos are fragile and precarious things.

In the second week of August 1992, we got a break. Harry Carlson, the company's vice chairman, met with two major Cleveland banks: National City Bank and Key Bank. They wanted to help. They immediately agreed to relax the covenants, provided that we seek a higher line of credit with a larger group of banks. They even promised to help us negotiate a new line of credit. One worry had been alleviated: we would be able to pay the bonus, albeit with borrowed money.

Meanwhile, the Europeans were demanding our first string—and they got it.

I left immediately for Europe.

-37-

European Shopping Spree

ALTHOUGH LINCOLN HAD operated manufacturing and marketing enterprises in Canada, Australia, and France for more than forty years, all three were independent of one another and had been essentially treated like colonies. Lincoln was primarily a US company, and its two main plants were—and still are—in the Cleveland area. It was our more recent, much bigger ventures overseas that were sinking us.

Since the deep US recession of the early 1980s, we had been talking about expanding abroad so that we wouldn't be so dependent on the domestic market. But Irrgang, who headed Lincoln from 1965 until 1986, had adamantly opposed the idea. Then in 1986, Irrgang died and was succeeded by George E. "Ted" Willis, and I was named President of North American operations.

Ted dreamed of Lincoln becoming a global power. Immediately after Ted became CEO, the company purchased Harris Calorific, a manufacturer of oxy-fuel cutting equipment with plants in Atlanta, Georgia, Italy, and the United Kingdom. When ESAB, a Swedish owned company, had marched in, purchasing two midsized manufacturers in the United States, we'd gotten a sharp wake-up call.

ESAB, already operating in the Far East and Latin America, obviously had global ambitions. Ted feared further incursions on the US market by ESAB–now able to use its non-US profits to buy up the American market. Due to Lincoln's extensive market share, antitrust laws prevented us from purchasing domestic competitors. Consequently, we decided to take the battle to ESAB's markets in Europe and Latin America. To offset ESAB's blatant purchase of US market share, our response would have to be quick–and substantial. It was.

During my tenure as President of Lincoln North America, Lincoln spent almost $325 million on expansion, a huge sum for a company of our size. The board (including me) believed that because we were so successful in the United States and had managed to transplant our incentive system to our Mexican operation, we could be successful anywhere.

Big mistake.

To our credit, Lincoln had successfully transferred our incentive system to our plant in Mexico City. That may sound surprising because the plant, which we bought in 1990, was unionized and piecework runs counter to the Mexican culture. To our credit, we had introduced the system gradually. The plant had about 175 workers, and we began by asking two of them to take a chance on piecework. We also put a net under them–that is, we guaranteed them a minimum income with no limit on the amount of money they could make.

As a result of changing their jobs to pay for performance, the two "volunteers" made more money performing the same job and they promptly showed their paychecks to the other workers. (Strange as that may seem, it's part of their culture.)

As soon as the higher wages were verified by their colleagues, more people asked to have their jobs transferred to the new system. It took about two years, but the entire operation eventually adopted piecework. If it is done slowly and properly, the system can be introduced into existing organizations or cultures where initially it might not seem to fit. Unfortunately, our success in Mexico had left us with a false sense of our own omnipotence.

The company had expanded rapidly. We had built three new plants in Japan, Venezuela, and Brazil. Lincoln had also purchased operations with eight plants in Germany, Norway, the United Kingdom, the Netherlands, Spain, and Mexico. To make matters worse, we had hit Europe at the peak of the market cycle and, consequently, had paid top dollar. We had bought an operation in Barcelona immediately following the 1988 Olympics, while the Spanish economy was booming and the construction market was incredibly strong. In less than a year, Spain had fallen into a deep recession.

In our naïveté, when we had examined the manufacturing operations of the foreign companies on our acquisition list, we had seen tremendous opportunities to reduce costs by applying our manufacturing expertise, equipment, and incentive system. We also knew that Lincoln could not afford to export consumables, namely certain electrodes and wire, from the United States. Consumables are a cutthroat commodity business. Had we exported those items, the shipping costs and duties alone would have priced us right out of the market.

We had also made some glaring errors in judgment. For example, without truly exploring the international culture, we had mistakenly assumed that our incentive system would be accepted abroad. Much to our horror, we discovered too late that the European labor culture was completely hostile to the piecework and bonus system. In fact, they were hostile to most things American (or so we were told).

Shame on us, we had bought into the idea that we could not export arc welding machines to most European countries, especially Germany, the major market in Europe. Our foreign distributors, along with our French and Norwegian managers, had hammered into us repeatedly that they could not sell products designed and manufactured in the United States due to the European bias toward their own goods. The managers insisted that it was impossible to establish a foothold in Germany unless we bought an established local player. Foolishly, we'd believed them.

In April 1991, we concluded our largest acquisition: certain assets of Germany's Messer Griesheim, including a plant just outside Frankfurt that manufactured arc welding machines, at a cost of more than $70 million. We were counting on the German economy to remain strong. Nobody foresaw the consequences of German reunification. The government's huge outlays to rebuild eastern Germany had led the inflation-wary Bundesbank to raise interest rates, one of several events that triggered the deepest recession in Europe since World War II.

Unfortunately, up to this point, my own involvement in the international arena had been minimal. As President, the only foreign operations that reported to me were our operations in Canada and Mexico. Before becoming President, my responsibility as Vice President of Sales had been limited to the United States.

As a director and as President, I did see the budgets and financial reports submitted by our foreign operations. By 1991, none of them, with the exception of those in Canada and Australia, were performing well. Profits had often been elusive at our French operation, which should have stood as a warning about global expansion. The operation in Brazil had been a sinkhole from the beginning, and the operations in Germany, Japan, Mexico, and Venezuela had never made money. The remaining entities were marginally profitable when we bought them, although none had world-class factories.

We were suffering the aftershock of an internal board of directors in a closely knit family business. Because several of the board members were Lincoln vice presidents and reported to the CEO, they were afraid to question his global initiatives until it was too late. The board, in lieu of challenging authority, held onto the myopic belief that our manufacturing expertise could easily bring the newly acquired operations up to our standards. This setup was nearly suicidal.

I felt as if I'd been handed the bridge on the *Titanic*.

-38-

Bonus: To Borrow or Not to Borrow?

THROUGHOUT ITS HISTORY, Lincoln had always been ultraconservative financially. Prior to our recent acquisitions, we'd had a cash reserve of more than $70 million and *no debt.* By 1990, we had not only used up that surplus but had taken on a small amount of debt. In 1992, our debt had soared to nearly $250 million—63 percent of equity!

Our directors—including me—had known that Lincoln would have to borrow to finance the acquisitions. What we had not fully considered, however, was that the very act of borrowing would be a major culture shock to our employees. Most people at Lincoln saw the taking on of *any* debt as reckless, a view with its roots deep in our incentive system.

Ever since the bonus had been introduced in 1934, management had explained to employees that it was a *cash*-sharing rather than a *profit*-sharing bonus. First we had to use the company's profits to pay dividends to our shareholders and to invest capital in Lincoln's future. Only after those needs had been met could we pay the bonus. *No cash* meant *no bonus.*

As soon as it became apparent that we had borrowed to finance the foreign expansion, employees became concerned. They could see it affecting their incomes, and as our level of debt increased, they grew deeply worried—and, in no uncertain terms, let senior management know it.

Lincoln had long preached and practiced open communication. Any employee who felt the need to speak to the CEO could see him. And many did. The same held true for other Lincoln executives; all had open doors. In this instance, employees—individually and through our twenty-seven-member advisory board—made their fears known. It all boiled down to one question,

"How can there be a cash bonus if we don't have any cash?"

Good point.

After taking over as CEO, I was faced with a terrible predicament. We could pay the bonus by taking the company deeper into debt, or we could announce that there would be no bonus and lose our people's trust—hence sacrificing the company's long-term competitive edge. It was a lose-lose proposition either way.

I thought long and hard about not paying the bonus—for approximately forty-seven seconds. Asking the people who had made the company successful to pay for the mistakes of management went against everything I believed in. I was reminded of something Jack Welch, former chairman of GE, once said (I'm paraphrasing): "Anyone can manage for the short term and anyone can manage for the long term; it's maintaining a balance between the two that's most difficult."

Yeah, *no kidding.* Except for the workers at the newly acquired Harris Calorific, all our US employees were eligible for a bonus. Because of the bonus and piecework pay, employees at our Cleveland-area factories and in our sales, distribution, and customer service centers throughout the United States act like entrepreneurs.

The bonus is payment for outstanding performance. Lincoln employees do perform—and not just in terms of high productivity and quality. Absentee and turnover rates are very low. In 1992, absentee rates were between 1.5 percent and 2.0 percent, and the turnover rate, including retirement but excluding new employees (people employed for ninety days or less), was 3.5 percent. When we have severe snowstorms, most of Cleveland shuts down, but Lincoln people make it in. (Did I mention attendance is also part of the bonus rating?)

Because our system draws out the best in people, they require very little supervision. The foreman-to-worker ratio at Lincoln's main US plants is 1 to 100. In a typical factory in the United States, the ratio is 1 to 25; in some auto assembly plants, it is 1 to 10. The savings from having relatively few supervisors helps the company pay the bonus. It was clear to me at that time that if we dropped the bonus, we would have to hire more employees because our productivity would go down. In other words, we couldn't try to save money by cutting out the bonus.

So where was the money going to come from?

-39-

"9-1-1, What Is Your Emergency?"

EUROPE. I HAD to be in Europe. With the company in crisis, I had to ignore my lack of extensive international experience and dive headfirst into the fray. But I was not the only one lacking significant international experience—none of our other senior managers had any either. Our chief financial officer, who was to join me on my first trip overseas, didn't even have a passport! We had to scramble to get him one at the last minute.

I held my first meeting with the CEOs of the European companies at the Hilton Hotel just outside Heathrow Airport. I thought it had been a good meeting. I'd received valuable input from all attendees. Due to continuing losses and vastly missed forecasts, we were in an emergency situation and everyone seemed eager to pitch in to help.

I assigned the Europeans the job of developing plans, complete with detailed sales strategies for turning around their businesses. The plans were to cover the fourth quarter of 1992 and all of 1993. The goal was to create profitable operations in 1993. The managing directors—along with our other foreign directors—were asked to submit their plans by early October.

After the meeting, I realized I needed some further clarification in one particular area. I put in a call to each of the managing directors. The shock came when I called France: "I'm sorry, but he is not here. Right after your meeting, he flew out of Heathrow to enjoy his annual six-week holiday in Italy."

What?

I took a deep breath and counted to one hundred. Or maybe it was one thousand; it certainly felt like it.

Once I stopped mentally hyperventilating, I finally choked out a few words to the receptionist, "Please contact him immediately. Tell him that unless he is back on the job within a week, he can stay 'on holiday' forever." He came back. I believe the French manufacturing facility has recently been closed.

In October we worked with J. P. Morgan to put together a ten-bank consortium that included National City Bank and Key Bank. True to their word, both banks stepped up to the plate by strongly supporting us in front of the other banks.

At the end of that month, we reported our third-quarter results. Our quarterly consolidated loss had increased to $9.2 million. Fortunately, the business plans for the foreign operations had arrived on schedule. We were able to show the ten banks that we had a strategy for dealing with the crisis and we began negotiations with them in November. We were seeking a credit line of $230 million to replace our existing line of $75 million—and we got it.

On December 4, 1992, we paid a $52.1 million bonus to our US workforce. The board also approved a shareholder dividend to keep our continuous record intact.

It was all borrowed money.

In January, we learned that our fourth-quarter consolidated loss was $19.8 million. That amount included a $7.4 million operating loss abroad and a $23.9 million restructuring charge. Fortunately, our US operations had reported a profit that softened the blow . . . a little.

To put the foreign operations in a stronger position to stage a rebound, we had decided to write off unneeded and obsolete machinery and questionable inventories. Although the foreign operations had not broken into the black by year's end, we were still hopeful that the turnaround plans would work. Our loss for the whole year was $45.8 million. The numbers were staggering.

In March, we signed the credit agreement with the ten banks. We thought we were over the hump. The European directors had assured us that the worst was behind them, and they seemed to be following their business plans.

But the business plans had not—and could not have—foreseen the deepening of the European recession. The plans were obliterated and the European results for the first quarter of 1993 were horrible: an operating loss of $14.4 million. Once again, the European managers had been overly optimistic and I had been overly trusting.

At least I thought that was what was happening.

In the spring of 1993, I finally chanced to learn why the European operations had chronically missed their sales and profit targets. Whenever I visited any of the European operations, I asked a multitude of questions and listened very carefully to their answers. I was learning to listen for problems that had not been fully disclosed. While I was in Barcelona, the Spanish CEO took me aside and let me in on a little secret. Well, actually it was a big secret.

Huge, in fact.

As Ted was finishing up his shopping spree across the pond, for some unknown reason he'd put the Norwegians in charge of Europe. The operating budget of the Norwegian management company was to be funded by the individual businesses in each country. The size of its budget would be based on the *forecasted* rather than the *actual* sales and profits of those businesses-- an odd set-up and a rather important little fact that no one had bothered to mention to me. Taking advantage of the situation in order to inflate the management company's own operating budget and pad individual pockets, their leaders had encouraged the other European businesses to submit ridiculously optimistic—rather than realistic—forecasts.

Fortunately, after we bought the Spanish company, the Spanish management team still retained a 10 percent equity interest. However, they were receiving pressure from Oslo to submit outlandish forecasts. The Spaniards knew full well that the payments to the European headquarters were based on forecasted rather than actual results. In essence, the Norwegians were bilking the other companies for personal gain. The Spanish CEO "resented" this practice and rightly so. He suggested I might want to address this issue.

Good God! As if things weren't bad enough, now I needed to deal with–I said some choice things here, but, well, I'm sure you don't need me to fill in the blanks. Suffice it to say, after a few brief expletives, I was rendered speechless.

Flying into action, I immediately confirmed the Norwegians', shall we say, "most unique and unorthodox business practices." The Spanish CEO was correct. I couldn't believe it. There was only one thing to do.

I closed the Oslo office and fired the occupants.

The Spaniards were shocked, as were the Norwegians (*damned Americans*). They weren't the only ones. Frankly, I was not only shocked by the Norwegians' avarice but stunned by the fact that the other European managers had never bothered to mention this "little issue." I think we all suffered culture shock in one form or another.

Once we'd passed around the smelling salts, the Spaniards thanked me and the other European managers were "relieved" that they could now work from forecasts that no longer crippled them financially. (The Europeans have a wonderful flair for understatement, don't they?) Wow. Well, who wouldn't be *relieved?*

Even though our hemorrhage across the pond had lessened to a slow drip, the crisis was far from over. In mid-May we received the numbers for April. They were devastating: Europe lost $8.2 million and the foreign operations as a whole lost $9.6 million. We seemed certain to violate the covenants in our new credit package. I wasn't sure how I would remain outwardly positive to our employees and board members, but I was determined to give it my best shot.

I'd been in the army long enough to realize that troops don't respond well to a morose and despairing commander.

-40-

Man Your Battle Stations! All Hands On Deck!

T HE WAY I saw it, we had two choices: we could resort to massive layoffs and cut executive salaries to save money, or we could make extraordinary efforts to increase revenues and profits. Several board members pushed the first option, putting tremendous pressure on me to take the traditional path and slash our workforce substantially. Although I understood their reasoning, I never seriously considered taking that route. Aside from turning my stomach ethically, I wasn't about to become the first Lincoln CEO to resort to layoffs since Harry Truman had occupied the White House. That's not how I solved problems.

I believed that downsizing violated everything Lincoln stood for. Our longtime covenant with our workers guaranteed them at least thirty hours of work per week. Downsizing could only result in the utter deterioration of morale, trust, and productivity. It's bad long-term business. If employees are just numbers, maybe it's easy to downsize. But when I walked into our cafeteria or onto the factory floor, I knew most of our people personally; I knew their families from our annual picnic. I regarded Lincoln's employees as resources, not liabilities.

I also didn't buy the argument that the only obligation that responsible corporations have to their employees is to guarantee *employability*, not employment. We invested an enormous amount in our people and ran dozens of training programs. *Our people* were trained to stay, not to be ready for dismissal.

Then I had an idea. A really BOLD idea.

Rather than downsize, why not *manufacture and sell our way out of this mess?*

God, that sounded so simple. Could it really *be* that simple?

No. Of course not. What was I thinking?

If we somehow managed to pull it off, *manufacturing and selling our way out of trouble* would certainly put a new twist on the term "crisis management."

I flashed back to our slogan on the wall: *The Actual Is Limited, The Possible Is Immense.* Left with few options, I had little choice but to find out just how immense "the possible" could be. I just hoped everyone else would be willing to follow me off the cliff.

Once I made the decision to forge ahead, I did the only thing I knew to do: I turned to our US employees for help.

I presented a twenty-one-point plan to the board that called for our US factories to boost production dramatically and for our sales force to sell our way out of the crisis. The plan called for the US operation to generate a pretax, prebonus profit of $52 million, instead of the $39 million in the original budget. I also offered to move to Europe to try to cauterize the wounds once implementation of the plan was under way. The board enthusiastically endorsed the plan and my offer.

I was shocked. I had expected more resistance. They must have been *really* worried.

In June, I appealed directly to our US employees: "We could do what other companies have done and downsize, but we're not going to. We're going to make the US company profitable enough to offset the losses abroad, remain within our bank covenants, and borrow the money again to pay the annual bonus in December. We're going to succeed by increasing the top line, not by cutting back and hurting our people."

The US company went into overdrive.

In small meetings with frontline employees, our executives explained the company's situation and our action plan. We explained our strategy to our employee advisory board and circulated the minutes of the session throughout our plants. We made a video and gave people copies to take home to watch with their families.

In the video, I was blunt. Management and the severe recession were to blame for the disastrous foreign expansion. "We blew it," I said. "Now we need you to bail the company out. If we violate the covenants, the banks won't lend us money. And if they don't lend us money, there will be no bonus in December."

I appealed not only to their loyalty but also to what James F. Lincoln had referred to as their "intelligent selfishness." If people believed they had a stake in their own future, they would be more willing to do what was necessary to help get the company out of trouble. We needed an all-out effort.

We then brought in our thirty-five district sales managers. We told them we expected them to come up with ideas and promotions that would sell the products we were gearing up to make. We also instituted a financial education program so that employees would understand that no money was being hidden from them and they could see exactly how much money the US operation needed to generate in order for us to be able to pay the bonus.

The all-out communication effort was critical—we needed everyone's total commitment. Rumors had already created anxiety and fear on the factory floor. We needed to give people an accurate picture of the company's problems and let them know that we had a plan to fight back. *Thank God* I had spent my years as President practicing Management

By Walking Around! The time I had invested in working with the folks in the plant proved more valuable than gold. We trusted each other.

My plan called for our US operation to increase sales from $1.8 million to $2.1 million per day. That was a tall order, given the still-soft US economy. Some in the rank and file said, "This is foolish. We're going to gear up, and by September, we'll all be on thirty hours per week." But I had faith in our sales force and knew they could sell everything we could produce. After all, they were *my guys*. The bigger challenge would be to boost production. We were operating at 75 percent to 80 percent of capacity. The plan implied a utilization rate of more than 100 percent.

We got moving immediately. The factory managers were asked to eliminate every bottleneck they could possibly find. The main bottleneck, they responded, was a shortage of people.

Really?

Most companies don't hire people during a financial crisis—but I refused to allow Lincoln to behave like most companies. We hired almost *one thousand*—a tremendous number for a company our size!

Unfortunately, it can take quite a while to learn how to run some of our equipment properly. It became apparent that with holidays and Lincoln's traditional two-week shutdown in August, we would not have enough capacity to meet the sales targets.

So I had another idea.

We started asking the veterans in the bottleneck areas to work over the holidays and postpone their vacations. They came through and we worked straight through our traditional August shutdown. About 450 people in the bottleneck areas gave up 614 weeks of vacation (the equivalent of almost twelve years!), with some people working seven days a week for months on end.

The employee advisory board worked closely with me along with the other executives. We used the board to apprise the workforce of our progress and maintain momentum.

I also turned to a handful of veteran rank-and-file workers who I knew would be completely straightforward with me. I asked them to let me know whenever there was a potential problem—bad attitudes, bottlenecks, parts shortages, etc. They knew how close we were to violating the covenants—we could not afford to wait for such information to filter up through the hierarchy.

We didn't have the luxury of time.

-41-

Transatlantic Triage

TRUE TO MY word, in early June 1993, I moved to England. I brought my wife, Shirley, and my executive assistant, Marylee Baller. We set up our European "headquarters" in a flat in Sunningdale, a suburb of London and an easy drive to Heathrow Airport. Marylee commandeered a spare room as her office and I took over the dining room. She moved into her own flat about a ten-minute walk from our "command center."

The US operation was left in the able hands of Fred Mackenbach, a Lincoln veteran (and my best friend during training) who had succeeded me as president. I didn't cut myself off totally; I received a host of faxes and phone calls each day from Fred and other managers in the United States. Fred largely ran the North American operations, while I focused on Europe, and Harry Carlson, our vice chairman, dealt with the other foreign businesses.

As soon as I arrived in Europe, I began holding group meetings with every major sales force that handled Lincoln's products. Every salesperson was asked to describe his territory, his customers, and precisely what he intended to do to get new business. It was the first time any of them had ever been required to commit themselves to a plan in front of other people.

During those months, as I met with the sales forces and managers and visited the factories, my hopes for turning around our businesses without a radical restructuring faded. Every factory was operating at fifty percent or less capacity.

The severity of the recession was horrifying. When I pushed managers to develop plans for increasing their market share, they brushed me off, saying, "The only way you increase market share is to buy another company. You *never* take an account from a competitor because they will retaliate and take one from you."

What?

As an American, I couldn't even wrap my brain around that comment.

Coupled with that ridiculous philosophy, my trip to the Messer Griesheim plant nearly threw me over the edge. People were *not working!* On one of my *preannounced* visits, I nearly tripped over three workers sleeping on the job.

What planet was I on?

I immediately approached the board. "We have *got* to get out of there. We've got to close the plant no matter what the cost. It's going to sink us." We had not yet tried to install the Lincoln incentive system in the factory. How naive we had been to believe that we could have.

Although I had not come up through manufacturing, I did realize that as engineering-minded as the Germans might be, even *they* couldn't make welding machines in their sleep.

The incentive system is transferable to some countries—especially to countries settled by immigrants, where hard work and upward mobility are ingrained parts of the culture. But in many other places, it won't easily take root. It is especially difficult to install it in a factory that has different work practices and traditions (like, for instance, *napping*).

For example, even though German factory workers are highly skilled and, in general, solid workers, they do not work nearly as hard or as long as the people in our Cleveland factory. In Germany, the average factory workweek is thirty-five hours. In contrast, the average workweek in Lincoln's US plants is between forty-three and fifty-eight hours, and the company can ask people to work longer hours on short notice—a flexibility that is essential for the system to work.

The lack of such flexibility was one reason why our approach would not work in Europe. Another was that in order to make a quality product, we have found, in our extensive time trials, that *productivity skyrockets when people stay awake.*

In September 1993, we were scheduled to demonstrate our products at a trade show in Essen, Germany. Traditionally, exhibitors had used the eight-day show as a venue for entertaining customers and conducting public relations, not for making sales. There were no laws or rules against selling, but tradition discouraged it.

I had other ideas—*tradition be damned!*

To spend a couple of million dollars on a trade show and not use it to land desperately needed sales seemed absurd. I saw the show as a sales opportunity, and during this crisis, we could not afford to pass up a single one.

I ordered three planeloads of our products from the United States and set an objective of selling 1,200 packages of semiautomatic welding equipment. Within those eight days, we sold 1,762! By testing the conventional wisdom, we discovered that excellent American-made products would sell in Germany—*very well,* in fact.

If that were true in Germany, it undoubtedly would be true elsewhere. We could close down some of our foreign machine-manufacturing operations and still compete in foreign markets.

I'm sure my little stunt at the Essen show was considered "extremely bad form" by European standards. I got the feeling that the Europeans regarded Lincoln with the same disdain the British Army had displayed toward the Colonials—during the days *when our militia had no uniforms and hid in trees.*

-42-

Big Enough to Fail

DURING MY FIRST nine months as CEO, the sheer severity and complexity of the crisis in Europe drove home the fact that the days when Lincoln could be run by one man were long gone. The company needed a bona fide management team. We needed more international expertise both in management and on the board. And we needed independent directors who would vigorously challenge the CEO. Even after my baptism by fire, I realized that I lacked in-depth international experience. With the continuing fiasco abroad, I felt overwhelmed and knew I needed help.

I had good reason to worry that if we ultimately had to take radical action overseas, our board might lack the knowledge and the stomach to do it. When the possibility of closing some of our operations had been raised, several directors exclaimed, "We just bought them! Why should we close them down this soon? We should fix them, not throw them out."

In my opinion, we needed new directors who did not have baggage from earlier decisions—people who would challenge long-standing assumptions and provoke or exasperate other board members—including me—if necessary. I went to the board's nominating committee. They agreed that we needed new blood and expertise on the board and in top management.

At the May 1993 shareholders' meeting, we elected three outside directors to replace three insiders who were vice presidents of the company. The new directors included Ed Hood, retired vice chairman and executive officer of General Electric, and Paul Lego, former chairman of Westinghouse, both stalwarts on the NEMA Board. At the same time, we invited Larry Selhorst, owner and CEO of American Spring Wire in Cleveland. A year later we brought on Henry Meyer III, president and chief operating officer of Key Bank. All four executives had strong international and/or financial experience.

We also brought in new talent at the top, even though it violated our long-standing policy of promoting from within. We were fortunate that in 1995, Fred Stueber, an attorney at Jones Day, agreed to sign on as vice president, general counsel, and secretary. Tony Massaro, a former Westinghouse executive who had been a member of Paul Lego's team, signed on as a consultant in 1993 to help me in Europe. He did a good job and consequently was named president of our European operations in January 1994. New blood began to fill in our thin management ranks.

In the fall of 1993, with the European arc welding industry mired in excess capacity, we drew up a radical restructuring plan. We scaled down operations in the United Kingdom, Spain, France, Norway, and the Netherlands. We closed the entire Messer organization and shut down manufacturing operations in Brazil, Venezuela, and Japan. (Even though we had built a plant in Japan, virtually no one would buy our products. Apparently, we had inadvertently "insulted" the Japanese by not having a Japanese partner. We had been *so* naive.) Our restructuring charge for the year was $70.1 million.

Ouch.

-43-

The Miracle on
St. Clair

FORTUNATELY, WE RECEIVED plenty of good news from the United States. John Stropki, general sales manager, inspired our sales force not only to achieve the $2.1-million-a-day sales target but to surpass it. By the end of 1993, in an heroic effort both on the factory floor and in the field, daily sales had climbed to $3.1 million, up from $1.8 million just two years prior—a 72 percent increase!

Now, in today's high-tech environment, those numbers may not give you goose bumps, but for a one-hundred-year-old company in an established, mature market, the figures were astronomical!

We would stay at that level throughout 1994 and beyond. Due to the dynamic leadership of Fred Mackenbach, our president; George Blankenship, manager of machine research and development; and David Fullen, vice president of machine manufacturing, we didn't miss a beat in production. Our workers are still proud of this accomplishment—and they should be. George is currently president and chief operating officer of Lincoln North America.

Our entire sales department gave a herculean effort. John Stropki, one of my original guys, did an outstanding job leading the troops. Needless to say, the Lincoln sales force was second to none. (Later, John would become the second CEO of Lincoln to rise through the sales department.)

Of course, many others played a big part. Our engineers came out with new products, such as a line for the light commercial and home market segments that we sold through Home Depot and Walmart. The doors to engineering had been thrown wide open and our new products both surprised and delighted our customers.

We also offered special promotions to our distributors that proved highly successful. Although they had a vested interest in seeing Lincoln survive the catastrophe, I will never forget the trust and heroic efforts of all involved. The years I had spent building relationships with their people paid off in spades.

David Nangle Jr., distributor sales manager, created some of the most creative and imaginative programs in the history of our distributor program. David is now president and CEO of the Harris Group.

In addition, public interest in the company grew through television specials. Dick Sabo launched a media blitz to introduce Lincoln's consumer product line to the general public, helping to raise our top line.

We also had some luck. Just as we were beginning to boost our production, the market started to revive—although nobody in the industry felt it yet. As a result, the upturn caught our competitors by surprise; they were still cutting back—while we were on the move.

At one of the European trade shows, I was chatting with an executive from one of our competitors. Under his breath, he said, "You know, if you raise prices just 5 percent, you could make an additional $50 million."

Hmmmm.

We were already cranked up and in a position to take market share.

Hmmmmmm.

If the price increases were *highly selective*, could we still take market share? Raising prices would certainly be a calculated risk (a HUGE calculated risk). The market was still sluggish.

I raised prices.

Our sales force made the new prices stick. And I never heard that we lost one account to our competition due to an undercut in pricing. Although I wasn't tracking competitive quotes at that time, I have often wondered if our competition may have increased prices too.

Hmmmmmmmm.

By October 1993, it was clear that Lincoln would be OK. Thanks to superhuman efforts in the factories and in the field, we were able to increase revenues and profits enough in the United States to avoid violating our loan covenants. The remarkable performance of the company's US workers put us in a solid position to ask the banks for new covenants in November. They approved them only two days before we were scheduled to pay the bonus.

On December 4, 1993, we paid a gross bonus of $55.3 million, again with borrowed money. Including the restructuring charge, we lost $38.1 million that year.

In the first half of 1994, we negotiated and carried out the plant closings. By mid-1994, the European and other foreign operations were in the black. Our new export strategy—which included selling American-made machines worldwide and rethinking which of our plants around the world could best serve a given market—was a smashing success. Moreover, in countries where we had closed operations, market share actually *increased!*

In 1994, we began rebuilding our balance sheet. I went to our US workers in July and carefully explained that we were going to begin investing in the future again. We had two priorities: reduce our debt and increase capital expenditures (which had been slashed during the crisis). Accordingly, we would have to reduce the individual bonuses paid that year.

With prosperity returning, our people understood the need to reduce our debt. In December, we again paid a collective bonus of over

$55 million: we didn't cut the total amount, but because of all the new hires, it was spread among more workers.

1994 was a better year all the way through. Our goals for the year were for our consolidated operations to achieve the highest sales, earnings per share, and return on investment in the history of our company–*and we met them.* We expanded our customer base and introduced new high-tech products. After the bonus payout, we earned $48.0 million for the year, *a one-year turnaround of almost $86 million.*

-44-

Unwinding Motors
(Oops!)

A S THE CRISIS was coming to a close, my three daughters joined us in Europe for a brief holiday. Nancy, my youngest (and a Motor Lady), sat me down for a serious chat.

Hmmm. . . . Motors? When was the last time I had given any serious thought to motors?

She informed me in no uncertain terms that there were problems with my ingenious program. Apparently, the Motor Ladies had not been a welcome addition to some of the district offices.

What?

With the company falling down around my ears, I hadn't been paying close attention to motors and it suddenly dawned on me that I had abandoned my plan to meet with the managers to properly launch the Motor Ladies.

As the father of three daughters, it never occurred to me that our people wouldn't immediately support my dazzling program. Shirley and I had raised our girls to be fiercely independent, and since they had all grown up climbing on the flux bags stacked in the Lincoln warehouse in Moline, they weren't afraid to get dirty. I didn't realize that many of our old-line industrial manufacturers and even a number of *my guys* took a dim view of women invading their traditionally male-dominated turf.

Because the Lincoln tech reps were trained to solve problems for customers, motors were never high on their priority list. Until Jack Roscoe instructed me to push motors to make up for deficiencies in welding sales, they hadn't been my favorite thing to sell either. I had assumed that the guys would welcome the chance to dump their motor sales on the Motor Ladies. I was wrong.

As it turned out, I had inadvertently stepped on their toes. Only a handful of the reps in the field were of any real help to the women once they arrived at their district offices. Apparently, the Motor Ladies suffered verbal abuse, discrimination in account assignments, and an overall lack of acceptance from the male sales force, not to mention heated intraoffice arguments about who would get sales and bonus credit for their motor sales.

Of course, none of *my guys* were talking. They would never openly criticize a program I had put together. Obviously, I should have talked to them up front and solicited their ideas. Hindsight, as always, is brilliant and infallible.

Frankly, the whole thing was a mess. I was a salesman and, crisis or no crisis, I'd forgotten to sell the sales force! Looking back, my lack of leadership was inexcusable. It just never occurred to me that my guys wouldn't automatically jump at the chance to make the program the success I knew it could be. I learned an important lesson:

Although vision is critical to the overall success of any endeavor, it is even more critical to <u>make sure those who are to execute it know what it is.</u>

While all this was taking place in the field, the company had entered into negotiations to purchase a cast-iron motor facility from General Motors in Dayton, Ohio. Once things had begun to improve for us financially, we'd agreed to purchase the plant with one caveat: we would install the Lincoln incentive system. GM's union workers had one thing to say: an emphatic *NO*. We couldn't believe it. They didn't even want to discuss it. Their outright refusal killed their jobs. GM closed the plant.

The plant closing actually worked in our favor. We went on to purchase the machinery from GM (at a much better price) and subsequently moved it to our Cleveland plant, with plans to completely modernize the manufacturing facilities. The cast-iron products complemented our steel frames, particularly in corrosive atmospheres, and increased our horsepower offering to 1,250 hp.

Nancy and I brainstormed a tremendous open house for the new operation with both the mayors of Euclid and Cleveland on the guest list. I knew they would be delighted to be invited and would praise Lincoln for investing in a new manufacturing plant in the depressed Euclid-Cleveland area.

I guess, in my haste to plug the gaping wounds in the *Titanic*, I had completely forgotten my promise to support the Motor Ladies. Nancy, in her infinite wisdom, demanded my undivided attention in England and she really let me have it. Although I didn't want to hear what she had to say, I can't say I didn't deserve it. Looking back, she'd been trying to tell me for months; I'd just been too busy flying around in my cape and tights to listen.

At the end of 1994, Shirley, Marylee, and I left England and moved back to Ohio. The crisis was over.

When I returned to Cleveland, I did make good on my promise to my daughter to dive into what was left of the motor program. Unfortunately, it was too little too late. Even with the grand opening of our new facility, with highly encouraging speeches given by both mayors, the motor program merely limped along. The damage had been done and there was too much bad blood between the sales force and the Motor Ladies.

So much for my motor ideas.

In hindsight, I still think the program had great promise. Unfortunately, it was launched at the worst possible time in the company's history. When the ship is sinking, you don't commit manpower to a product line that accounts for less than 15 percent of your bottom line and expect people to line up behind you. And they didn't.

At one point, I was receiving so much conflicting feedback that I decided to take all the emotion out of the equation (including my own) and seek outside counsel. I contacted a friend at McKinsey Consulting in Cleveland to lead a discussion of Lincoln's position in the motor industry. He agreed to spend an afternoon with us, and I looked forward to receiving an objective analysis.

We gathered the major players together from engineering, manufacturing, and sales—anyone and everyone who had anything to do with motors. After three hours of intense debate, there was no question that we were *completely divided*. I had never seen anything quite like it. We zeroed in on the following issues:

- Loyalty to John C. Lincoln's first product was dwindling.

- JF's notion that motors were a good hedge against the welding industry was suspect (I'd proven that in Moline).

- Motors were considered a distraction of time, resources, and management talent from our core business.

- Lincoln lacked the critical mass to compete with the Baldors and Emerson Electrics of the world in a highly competitive and diverse market.

Everyone knows that a house divided cannot stand. Never one to give up, I encouraged people to do their best and "give it the old college try."

It didn't work.

Although profitable, motors merely hobbled along. Perhaps my attachment to JF and my past immersion in motors blinded me just a little with regard to motors.

Perhaps.

I'm sure Irrgang was looking down at me, cigar in hand, having a good laugh. "Not so easy to let one go, is it, Don?"

After I retired, I can't say I was surprised to hear Ed Hood say, "Now let's get rid of the motor division." They sold it fairly quickly, although at a considerable loss.

So much for my motor theories.

The Motor Ladies were terminated and I believe certain members of management heaved a sigh of relief.

The State of Ohio didn't comment.

Hmmmm.

-45-

Wall Street Warriors

BY 1995, THE crisis was over. The company was making healthy profits, particularly in North America. Various board members and I were debating a public offering. Several Lincoln family board members questioned the advantages of the offering carrying voting privileges. Up until this time, Lincoln had remained almost exclusively a privately held company. Our stockholders consisted of employees and Lincoln family members, a rare fact for a billion-dollar operation.

There were two reasons to go public at that time: first, although the future looked bright and we really didn't need the cash, if we were going to do it at all, now would be a good time. Second, there was no open market for stock held by employees, the Lincoln family, and the Lincoln Foundation. The majority stockholders were David Lincoln, his sister (Lillian Lincoln Howell, also a Pomona graduate), and the John C. Lincoln Foundation. David was strongly in favor of the offering as he and other family members could attach their holdings to a public sale.

Russ Lincoln, a family member and board member, wanted to ensure that the Lincoln family would still have a strong voice with respect to dividend payments after going public. I sold the idea of a *nonvoting* stock to the board. We had established a good relationship with Merrill Lynch and went ahead with an initial public offering for a nonvoting issue. (Pretty good sales pitch on my part.)

Our new chief financial officer and I put on multiple presentations in major cities including Cleveland, Chicago, New York, London, Glasgow, Paris, San Francisco, and Denver. Merrill Lynch provided us with an executive jet for our domestic flights, and we flew back and forth to Europe on the Concorde, a far cry from what I was used to at Lincoln.

We raised over $80 million for Lincoln and over $30 million for the Lincoln family. When we finished, David Lincoln, a man of few words, called me and simply said, "Thanks."

Lincoln Electric is listed on the NASDAQ as LECO.

-46-

The 64.4-Million-Dollar Question

A T THE END of 1995, Lincoln was scheduled to pay out the largest bonus in the history of the company. It was our one hundredth anniversary and we as a company had been celebrating *The Miracle on St. Clair* (our street address). Since we had risen out of the ashes to record sales and profits, the employees naturally expected huge bonuses. Some began to believe they would receive 100 percent of their yearly compensation at bonus time (to match our one hundredth anniversary). After all, we had hit $1 billion in sales and were about to pay out a bonus totaling $64.4 million.

There were only two problems: First, several of our outside board members didn't want to pay a large bonus. In fact, some lobbied not to pay one *at all*. I had to fight just to get it to 55 percent. Second, even though our total payout was the highest ever, it would be split between a greater number of employees, thus lowering each individual's total amount.

I understood why the employees in the factory expected a large bonus—they'd worked their tails off. And I would have liked nothing better than to accommodate them. However, it would have been fiscally irresponsible of me to do so and nearly impossible for the board to justify a higher payout given the economic waters we had just navigated and the need for caution as we looked ahead.

Try telling that to a cafeteria full of angry workers.

Then I had an idea.

I split our employees into groups and held separate meetings to explain the company's position. I addressed groups at both our Euclid and Mentor facilities. I knew they had busted their tails to help us out of the mess we'd been in and they had a right to speak to me directly.

I learned an important lesson in those meetings: *never give up the microphone to an angry employee.* I made that mistake once. I watched one guy get so carried away that I thought he would incite a riot.

Lincoln employees are not shy about voicing their complaints, especially to management. I had caught wind that certain employees were staging a worker demonstration and were threatening a UAW union vote. Needless to say, I was hoping to head that one off at the pass. Once people realized I was actually willing to listen to them, they calmed down somewhat. A few of our factory workers even asked what they could do to boost sales, thus increasing the bonus pool. Wow. At that moment I knew, in every fiber of my being, what Abraham Lincoln meant when he penned the words "last full measure of devotion."

I'd like to say that my meetings were a resounding success and that I never heard another word. However, that was not the case. On more than one occasion, I was physically threatened. I couldn't blame the employees for being upset, and there were several that were real cause for concern. Although I hoped I wouldn't have to use it, I kept a baseball bat next to our front door at home for months.

-47-

Out from
Behind the Mask

THROUGHOUT MY TENURE as President, and later as CEO and Chairman of the Board, I worked quietly to bring Lincoln Electric more to the forefront of the Greater Cleveland community. As a manufacturing company, Lincoln's reputation was second to none, but as a community-minded organization, we were known for being, well, *cheap*. And we were, as far as our community was concerned: we poured all our money back into the company and employees.

To give Lincoln some much needed visibility, I joined Cleveland Tomorrow, a group of the city's elite businessmen who had been responsible for saving the city of Cleveland from bankruptcy under Mayor Dennis Kucinich. (No comment).

In addition, I accepted the challenge of chairing the capital campaign to build Hope Lodge, a refuge for out-of-town cancer patients under intensive treatment at either University Hospitals or the Cleveland Clinic. Hope Lodge is thriving today and is a wonderful asset to the medical community.

It was a time in which I proved that it really is possible to *do well and do good* simultaneously. Give it a shot. Really, there's no other feeling like it.

-48-

Backfire

I'D HAD SEVERAL conversations with Paul Lego prior to his coming on board at Lincoln. He stayed on for six years and was a real driver, particularly in regard to management succession. From the time he joined Lincoln, he encouraged me to hire Anthony Massaro, a cohort from Paul's Westinghouse days. I'd had misgivings about hiring Tony, though I couldn't exactly put my finger on why. However, I was so busy bailing out the boat with every bucket I could get my hands on, I took Paul's advice and hired him anyway.

It was clear to me from the start that Tony wanted my job. He just didn't want it at that particular moment. Who did? I wasn't even sure I wanted it.

Unfortunately, in my naïveté, I had been under the mistaken impression that the new outside directors were there to help me turn things around. However, rather than acting as advisors, they behaved more like the CEOs and executives they had been in their former companies. Almost everyone wanted to run things. Talk about too many cooks in the kitchen! Once again I was reminded to be careful what I ask for.

Looking back, the situation was actually kind of comical—all those egos (including mine) banging into one another, vying for position. If that can happen in a small boardroom in Euclid, Ohio, it's no wonder nothing gets accomplished in Washington, DC.

I knew I was safe as long as the company was in trouble. I don't think there were many sailors vying for the captain's chair on the *Titanic*. But as soon as the ship started to right, I could feel certain sights zeroing in on my back. Once the company was back in the black, who wouldn't want my job? Hell, *I* wanted my job! Compared to surviving the tsunami I had inherited, running a Fortune 500 company that's making money is akin to sailing a ship on a calm sea—almost.

I have no doubt that certain board members had little intention of waiting for me to voluntarily retire before putting one of their own at the helm. Looking at the previous Lincoln CEOs' track records, I'm sure they figured my successor would be waiting a very long time.

They were right.

I had no intention of retiring. After bringing Lincoln back from the brink of disaster, I was looking forward to continuing to lead the company I had worked so hard to save. In my opinion, from the time Tony came on board, I believe he and Paul had every intention of replacing me as CEO as quickly as they could (once we were back in the black, of course). And they did.

Tony had Paul as his management succession advocate, leading the way on the board. Conventional wisdom led Paul to initiate mandatory retirement at age sixty-five for all executives. I was already sixty-seven. Hell, I was just getting warmed up! Of course the board could make exceptions—and they did for me for one year. After my year was up, they asked me to retire. I was sixty-eight. By bringing in the outside directors, I had unwittingly become the catalyst of my own destruction.

This move was a prime example of "be careful what you wish for." I had always thought Lincoln should have some type of mandatory retirement. JF and Irrgang had held on forever, and if it hadn't been for pressure from his wife, Rolande, I'm sure Ted would have stuck around longer. (Well, maybe not. Maybe he left before the news of the mess we were in hit the street—or the Lincoln cafeteria.)

As a company, Lincoln had suffered at the hands of this lingering policy by the three previous CEOs, resulting in stagnation and potential bankruptcy. However, although I realized we should implement some type of term limitation, I had no intention of starting the program in the first year of my turn at bat. Hell, in my opinion, the clock on my tenure as CEO shouldn't have officially started until *after* the turnaround. Now that we were right side up, I was finally having some fun!

Over the years, I have heard through the grapevine that aside from younger bucks wanting my job, once Humpty Dumpty had been put back together, the board began to think in more conservative terms once again. A number of board members were older and, under normal circumstances, completely risk-averse. But these last few years had not been "normal circumstances." As long as we were in real trouble, they gave me a lot of latitude. What else could they do? We didn't have a lot of time to argue.

In my own defense, my ideas, unorthodox as they may have been, had righted a sinking ship. During the turnaround, no one had been laid off, dividends had been paid to our shareholders, and we had paid out a record bonus in overall dollars. The company had risen like a phoenix from the ashes. What was the problem?

Obviously, crisis management is an animal unto itself. People tend to take more chances when their basic survival is at stake. *We* did. However, in the long run, once the crisis is over, those same people tend to fall back into their comfort zones, and the Lincoln board of directors was certainly more comfortable with more conservative management practices than those that I had employed to save the company. In addition, they now had outside stockholders to consider.

When I think about the situation now, if I add my unexpected methods to my age at sixty-eight, factor in a new board with traditional management styles, coupled with new outside stockholders, and multiply by the number of people who would have loved to have my job, the answer I come up with is *Get Rid of Don*, of course.

My only consolation was the fact that the company did offer me a paid consulting agreement for seven years. I was awarded the title of Chairman Emeritus and provided an executive assistant and a very nice OUTSIDE office (for three years) as long as I signed a seven-year noncompete. There was one point I could never reconcile: if they thought I was so old, obsolete, and expendable that I couldn't do my job, why did the noncompete last until I was *seventy-five?*

Here is what I think—or at least what I like to think. I think I was hired and "retired" for all the same reasons. I believe that J. F. Lincoln saw something in me that spring day in Boston in 1953: perhaps my potential, perhaps a younger version of himself. Whatever it was, we had an immediate connection that was, at least for me, to last my entire career and beyond. I think the new breed at Lincoln may not understand either one of us. I'm not sure they feel they need to.

I truly believe that the new board believed that by getting rid of me, they would rid the company of the last vestiges of JF and his stubborn adherence to a unique yet highly controversial management style. I was the last direct link to J. F. Lincoln, his incentive management system, and guaranteed employment.

I have to admit, I *had* written a few editorials that did not particularly ingratiate me with other corporate CEOs and possibly with a few of my own board members who had been longtime members of what I had dubbed the "layoff fraternities." If the company could rid themselves of Don Hastings, they would eliminate any remaining ties to the past.

And they did.

-49-

Making Enemies

I N FEBRUARY 1996, I was invited to speak at the famous City Club of Cleveland. I've included a few of the ideas here that no doubt helped spark the rift within our board.

My speech was entitled "Guaranteed Employment: A Practical Solution for Today's Corporations."

Although my talk was a hit with the audience, it didn't make me many friends in the business community, especially with members of the so-called "layoff fraternities," which included a couple of our outside board members.

Here's an excerpt:

> There are two words in the English language that, when uttered sequentially, will cause most executives to choke: *guaranteed employment*. They feel it is an unnecessary constraint on their modus operandi. Well, if slashing their workforces in tough times is their modus operandi, then perhaps it is.

I've been looking forward to coming here today to discuss the ideas of guaranteed employment and incentive pay and to tell you a little bit about what goes on at Lincoln and why President Clinton invited me to join a conference on corporate citizenship.

The invitation letter from the White House said, "This conference will bring together the President and his key economic team with a diverse group of business leaders from all areas of the country, to discuss what American business can do to increase economic opportunity and security for their employees and their families in a way that is good for business and for economic growth."

There were many good things that happened at the conference. The President proposed tax incentives for employer-funded education. And we heard many good stories about the value of things like on-site day care, health care benefits, flexible work schedules, and training programs designed to improve *employability*.

All these are worthwhile goals. But I had a feeling that none of them came close to being a recipe for relieving the stress, the uncertainty, the anxiety that plagues so many people today. Let's not kid ourselves: those stresses and uncertainties can be a major drain on productivity as well as a force undermining families and communities.

The real issue is how to give people some guarantee that their good work today will result in having a job tomorrow. When I raised the issue with President Clinton, he brushed me off, saying he did not fully agree. "People make mistakes," he said, "and sometimes when senior management has diversified too much, a division or two might have to be cut off, resulting in layoffs."

Good God! Here was the President of the United States (a Democrat, no less) *defending layoffs!*

Then John Snow, chairman of CSX Corporation, piped up and said, "We must start with the reality that corporations cannot guarantee anyone a lifetime job any more than corporations can have a guarantee of immortality." John Snow later became Secretary of the Treasury.

Out of the approximately one hundred attendees, there was only one other who verbally supported my comments.

There's no doubt about it: American business wants the power to treat their workers as costs and be able to reduce those costs whenever they deem it necessary. Although there is no question there is very little support for my position, I strongly believe that good management should treat their workers as people, not simply costs, and use creative and innovative ideas and practices to save them from the devastation of layoffs. It can be done. We did it!

Thinking ahead and having creative solutions is what management is all about!

Many graduate business schools study the Lincoln Electric Company. It still amazes me to hear so-called "enlightened minds" call the program antiquated, difficult to implement, unrealistic or, in extreme cases, even a tad *barbaric*. Funny, my generation would have simply called it *good business*.

Skeptics especially love to criticize guaranteed employment or employment security of any kind. They say that the practice is unnecessarily limiting, that it breeds complacency in the workplace, and that it places undue financial strain on the company. These statements are ridiculous.

In our layoff-driven business climate, they see any form of employment security as potentially crippling and an unnecessary financial burden. I find it ironic that the bulk of the people who loudly criticize guaranteed employment are, in fact, *tenured professors*. If the terms guaranteed employment and employment security are to be shunned, should we just call the concept *tenure*?

Based upon my experience at Lincoln, I believe massive layoffs are, in general, a sign of *catastrophic failure* on the part of management. Even the notion of employability, which, I guess, means training people for the eventuality of being fired, is like handing the football to a running back without any blockers for protection.

I think it is time we take a hard look at what is going on. We need to find creative solutions to replace the notion that downsizing is a cure-all for a company's ills. It is management's responsibility to find these solutions, to plan ahead, to be flexible enough to respond to any new situation.

As I stated previously, *that's what management is all about.*

(As you can imagine, I wasn't exactly rising to the top of the How to Win Friends and Influence People category with my peers).

-50-

Ethics? Where Is the Profit in Ethics?

B ELOW IS AN abridged version of an article I wrote for the editorial page of *The Cleveland Plain Dealer* on May 17, 1996.

Obviously, I was on a roll–and *not* aligned with conventional thinking.

The Value of Ethics

By Donald F. Hastings

Recent studies by graduate business schools have found that many future business and professional leaders express no concerns whatever about occasionally lying, cheating, or bending the truth, if they believe the result of their dissimulation will benefit their organizations or, more particularly, themselves.

"Ethics?" these young people ask. "Where is the profit in ethics?" This is an alien attitude to someone of my generation. Of course, it should be an alien attitude to everyone in business or government, no matter his or her age, level of education, or position.

(I have to add that I've been completely shocked to witness the obvious and disgraceful lies, corruption, and illicit behavior demonstrated by our elected officials! How much longer can we afford to allow corrupt politicians to *masquerade* as statesmen?)

The value of ethics has always been a fundamental tenet of my business life, as well as the organization for which I work. In fact, I joined the Lincoln Electric Co. in 1953 as a young, entry-level sales trainee after hearing the company's longtime CEO speak eloquently about personal responsibility, accountability, and ethical behavior in the business world.

I took his words to heart and have never regretted it. Aside from the satisfaction you garner from knowing that you are doing the right thing, there is indeed a dollar-and-cents value to maintaining high ethical standards in business. I have found, as have many others, that emphasizing open and honest relationships among managers, employees, customers, and shareholders pays off, ultimately, in a successful and profitable organization.

Over the years, a company policy of ethical behavior will almost always engender a level of mutual respect and a reservoir of trust between management and workers. Trust is a commodity more valuable than gold.

To illustrate the value of such a reservoir of trust, I need look no further than my own experience as Chairman and CEO. My tenure in office was exactly twenty-four minutes when I received word telling me that our losses in our European operations were much worse than previously reported. In fact, the drain was so substantial that we would have to declare a loss—the first annual loss in our history—and the crisis threatened to sink the entire company.

Declaring losses in both 1992 and 1993, we were under pressure to consider curtailing our famous bonuses to employees. I felt strongly that such a move would prove fatal to the relationship of trust between management and workers.

Consequently, we took the unprecedented step of borrowing the money to pay the bonuses–$44 million in 1992 and $55 million in 1993.

At the same time, we were working hard to *manufacture and sell* our way out of the crisis. Sales and distribution people went on a marketing blitz. The orders they generated resulted in record domestic sales, which challenged our production people as never before.

Their response to the challenge was a testament to the value of a corporate philosophy of ethical dealings at all levels of an operation. Workers identified and eliminated dozens of bottlenecks in the manufacturing process. Key employees voluntarily deferred a total of 614 weeks of vacation. Many worked holidays and some worked seven days a week to fill the orders that were pouring in.

Ultimately, we overcame the crisis, and today have solidly returned to profitability. We have added hundreds of employees. In 1995 we paid $64.4 million in bonuses–and not just to top management!

None of this would have been possible without tapping the reservoir of trust we worked so long and hard to maintain.

A company philosophy based on fairness, honesty, and trust may seem old-fashioned to today's management gurus, but it has proven its worth many times for many organizations.

What, then, is the value of ethics in business?

Look at our bottom line and judge for yourself.

The reviews in the Cleveland business world were mixed and the article seemed to add to certain board members' belief that I was completely out of step with current business values and practices. I didn't care.

At least I could sleep at night.

NO ONE would go hungry on my watch.

188

-51-

The Purge

WITH AN OUTSIDE board of directors and outside investors to consider, the board had an excuse to return to traditional Wall Street management practices, which meant highlighting short-term quarterly profits rather than emphasizing long-term value. And they have done just that. And to their credit, quite profitably, I might add. (It kills me to admit that.)

Over the next year, the "purge of J. F. Lincoln" went well beyond me. The new regime also saw fit to eliminate a number of competent and dedicated vice presidents and managers I had trained who had been instrumental to Lincoln's success. This regime, it appears, did not want to compete with any so-called "disciples" of Don Hastings, so they found a way to shed as many of *my guys* as they safely could. I won't name them.

I have been told by many former employees, especially my guys, that I was the last remaining link to J. F. Lincoln. They have thanked me for that and thanked me for the opportunity to work for such a unique company under "truly inspired" management. I carry the title of Chairman Emeritus of the Lincoln Electric Company with great pride.

I must admit that I have had to make peace with what happened at the end of my career. It wasn't easy. This book has helped. Coupled with a six-year stint with the American Welding Society Foundation, I spent a total of fifty years in the welding industry. At eighty-five, as I watch today's corporate CEOs becoming younger and younger, I can understand why I was asked to leave at sixty-eight . . . *almost.*

I worked for Lincoln Electric for forty-four years. I found my place in the world in 1953 and never looked back. And I don't regret one minute of the experience. I have been blessed with two great love affairs in my life—one personal and one professional—that lasted my entire career and beyond. Thank you, J. F. Lincoln. And thank you, Shirley Tedder Hastings.

How many people get to say that? Not many, I suspect.

52-

On the House

S INCE MY HANDS were tied for seven years under a noncompete (and I was sixty-eight years old), I offered my hand to the nonprofit world. I had a ball! In the years following my retirement, I held the following positions:

Chairman, Board of Governors, National Electrical Manufacturers Association (NEMA), Washington, DC–two years

Chairman, Harvard Business School Global Alumni Conference, Cleveland, Ohio–three years

Board member, Harvard Business School Alumni Board, Boston, Massachusetts–three years

Board member, American Welding Society Foundation, Miami, Florida–six years

Chairman, Cleveland Council on World Affairs, Cleveland, Ohio–three years

Chairman, Cleveland World Trade Center, Cleveland, Ohio–two years

Executive committee, Greater Cleveland Growth Association, Cleveland, Ohio–three years

Board member, Salvation Army, Cleveland, Ohio–two years

Board member, Case Western Reserve University, Weatherhead School of Management, Cleveland, Ohio–three years

Board member, Lake Erie College, Painesville, Ohio– two years

President, Harvard Club of Naples, Florida–two years

During those years, I was busy. In addition to the organizations I served, I also gave a number of talks to various universities around the country (including Harvard, MIT, Notre Dame, and Cal Tech), counseled young professionals, and served on several corporate boards.

Yes, it was fun. *But not as much fun as running a profitable billion-dollar corporation.*

-53-

"The First Thing We Do, Let's Kill All the Lawyers"

—William Shakespeare,

Henry VI

I WASN'T GOING TO include this chapter in the book because, quite frankly, the entire subject turns my stomach. However, these types of situations are so much a part of the fabric of modern day life (and business) that I felt I needed to say something. While I was heavily involved in the nonprofit sector, I got saddled with a front row seat to the American legal system, a far cry from jurisprudence. Ugh. It was an eye opening experience.

At that time, there were two major lawsuits against Lincoln.

First, shortly after the Northridge earthquake in Southern California, lawyers descended on Lincoln. The quake had devastated numerous buildings and structures. The insurance companies had taken the brunt of the monetary hit and their lawyers were sniffing out anyone with deep enough pockets to sue for reimbursement.

During the earthquake, many structures made from wood or concrete completely collapsed. The remaining structures made from welded steel sustained some damage, but *none* saw catastrophic failure and *all* remained erect. Per usual, that made no difference to the lawyers. Since Lincoln was the major supplier of welding wires to the construction industry, and I happened to be CEO at the time of the quake, I was called to testify in numerous depositions and trials.

Fortunately, I was backed up technically by Duane Miller, a LeTourneau University engineer in our Weldtech department. His expert testimony wowed the jury and Lincoln was exonerated. The entire exercise was a supreme waste of time, effort, and money—unless you were one of the lawyers, of course.

The second lawsuit involved manganese. After the asbestos/cancer lawsuits had run out of steam, the legal profession zeroed in on the welding industry. They claimed that over exposure to manganese fumes caused amyotrophic lateral sclerosis (ALS), a.k.a. Lou Gehrig's disease. Most welding materials do contain manganese to increase the strength of the welds. During the welding process, smoke is released into the atmosphere. If there is not proper protection or ventilation, the welders can inhale the fumes. If inhaled in large enough amounts, manganese can cause tremors similar to ALS or Parkinson's disease.

However, without manganese in the consumables (which would violate all sorts of regulations), let's just say I wouldn't want to be up in a penthouse on a windy day unless the builders had reverted back to using rivets or bolts. (Considering the fact that many of my depositions were taken in law offices ensconced in skyscrapers, I'm sure the attorneys on both sides were happy the welding industry used manganese).

Lincoln's specialty high-manganese electrodes and wires do carry severe warning labels about the dangers of manganese. The good news is that the courts have recognized this precaution. However, the trial lawyers have tried and, I understand, are still endeavoring to prove that even low manganese levels in mild steel products are problematic. They claim the warning labels on the cartons are not sufficient to protect the welder.

In my view, this is absolute nonsense. Welders are highly trained and educated in their field. Common sense would tell you that welders actually have a much better chance of electrocuting themselves or falling off bridges and skyscrapers than becoming ill from manganese fumes.

Just kidding . . . sort of.

As a product of my generation, I don't understand the current movement to substitute litigation for common sense. But then again, I'm not a lawyer. My generation was raised to ask "What can I do?" not "Whom can I blame?"

Litigation is expensive in many ways. It's no secret that huge settlements lead to financial hardship and can potentially put companies out of business and cost people their jobs. Litigation brings verdicts. Verdicts bring regulation. Regulation restricts the freedom of the individual.

If we want the freedom to choose, we must be willing to take full responsibility for our choices. It's that simple. All this miscellaneous grandstanding is ludicrous. As a society, we are heading down a very dangerous path.

OK, I'll get off my soapbox now. And I *really commend* the lawyers who refrain from engaging in these sorts of practices.

Although the trial lawyers banded together to attack Lincoln, most of the cases have either been dismissed or awarded to Lincoln Electric. I'm happy to report that I haven't been called to testify since I turned eighty.

Hmmmmm.

Maybe I have a case for age discrimination.

-54-

The Mistake on the Lake

THOSE FIRST SEVEN years after I left Lincoln, I thoroughly enjoyed my time on the various boards and I met some great people. They were a welcome relief to the hours and hours I spent in depositions and courtrooms.

However, while I have great respect for the nonprofit sector, the only office I held that even vaguely resembled my former life in business was chairing the Harvard Business School Global Alumni Conference. Like manna from heaven, I was handed the opportunity to be a salesman again.

I had been a member of the Harvard Business School Club of Northeast Ohio since arriving in Cleveland in 1970. But because I traveled constantly (and missed out on almost everything), it came as a shock when several members invited me to lunch at the Union Club in Cleveland in 1997. After the salad, they asked me to chair a potential HBS Global Alumni Conference in Cleveland in 2001.

Cleveland? Really? The past conferences had been held all over the world: Paris, Tokyo, Chicago, Hong Kong, San Francisco, and New York, with the upcoming conference scheduled for Cape Town, South Africa, the following autumn. And these guys thought Cleveland should get a shot at it. I loved the audacity of their idea—and the challenge.

I jumped at the chance. Our group immediately applied to the alumni board in Boston to be considered. They gave us a tentative OK, but we could hear their snickers echoing throughout Northeast Ohio.

At the event in Cape Town, the alumni board announced that the following year the conference would be held in Berlin to commemorate the tenth anniversary of the fall of the Berlin Wall. The audience stood and cheered!

Once they calmed down, the board announced that they were considering Cleveland for 2001. The audience broke out in raucous, uncontrollable laughter!

They'd thought it was a joke! The Mistake on the Lake, the river that caught fire, an abandoned steel town, blah, blah, blah. I'd heard it for years from late-night talk show hosts.

Due to the response the Cleveland announcement had made on the crowd, the alumni board summoned our group to Boston. They wanted us to justify Cleveland as a choice to be *honored* with the 2001 conference.

Oh, boy. Here we go.

Our group made a pact not to become defensive. Now that I think about it, what an odd pact—although if one is from Cleveland, one does get used to that sort of thing.

Then I had an idea.

I had a pretty good feel for what we were up against. I'd faced similar audiences in the cafeteria at Lincoln. I knew from experience that a room full of calm, happy, open-minded people is an easier sell than a semihostile, close-minded crowd. Sooo . . . let's make them calm, happy and receptive.

Hmmmm.

Chocolate.

For over fifty years, I lived in a house filled with women. In that time, I have personally witnessed the astounding and awe-inspiring power of chocolate to soothe the savage beast. Since obviously offering a valium lick to the board members was out of the question, before we began our presentation to the Boston crew, we handed out chocolate. *Really good chocolate.*

They devoured it. A minute or two later, as I watched the committee members visibly relax, I took the floor. I opened by issuing a challenge, "How could you ever consider the Mistake on the Lake? How could you choose a city where the river burns or the mayor's hair catches fire?"

The room filled with laughter and the shaking of heads. I could hear what they were thinking, "Is this guy serious? Did he really go to school here?"

I pressed on. "All that aside, Cleveland, in fact, is now a revitalized monument to the Industrial Revolution. For close to a century, the city thrived because it manufactured *things*–things that the rest of the world needed and wanted. Although Cleveland has been masked by many problems over the years, it remains a hidden jewel due to its hardworking, dedicated, and highly ethical population. It's also made one *helluva* comeback. How could you NOT consider a city like that?"

I'd finally gotten their attention.

In addition to expounding upon the virtues and revitalization of the city of Cleveland, I assured the alumni board that we really were serious --we would put on a spectacular conference if they gave us the chance.

Soothed by serotonin (and our sincerity), they voted unanimously in favor of Cleveland for 2001. Although they obviously liked my pitch, I will always revere the mystical power of the cocoa bean. Looking back at my "mandatory retirement," had I not been preoccupied with dodging bullets, I would have bought the entire Lincoln succession committee a crate of Godiva truffles.

As luck would have it, the laughter that Cleveland received in Cape Town actually fueled our efforts and was a great lead in for our fund-raising efforts. You'd be surprised at how people rally behind their civic pride—especially when their city is the brunt of worldwide jokes. Suddenly, everyone was on our side.

Our primary sponsors came from major corporations whose executives either had an MBA from Harvard or had attended the business school's Advanced Management Program. As we progressed, word got out and many other alums joined our efforts with cash contributions. Even Mayor Michael White pitched in to help us by creating a ten-minute video personally inviting the graduates to come to Cleveland.

Next stop: Berlin. A Cleveland fearsome foursome (including me) set off for the new Germany accompanied by Joan McCarthy, our club administrator. Joan set up a phenomenal display in the Hilton Hotel lobby in East Berlin and we proudly showed our video at the conference.

Our ultimate goal was nine hundred attendees—the maximum number of concert goers the internationally renowned Cleveland Orchestra could accommodate at Severance Hall. As a kickoff, we offered the seven hundred and three Berlin alums a discount if they signed up for Cleveland before they left the conference. We signed one hundred thirty-eight.

We blew Boston's mind with our final ad in the *Harvard Business Review*: SOLD OUT! Yes, Cleveland. We even had a waiting list!

An evening performance by the world famous Cleveland Orchestra was just the beginning of the goodies we had scheduled for the alums. We rocked the house at the Rock and Roll Hall of Fame with a live performance by the Beach Boys. We also treated the attendees to a sunset cruise on Lake Erie, trips to museums, professional sporting events, ringside seats to an open-heart surgery at the Cleveland Clinic, a tour of Lincoln Electric (the highlight, of course), and ongoing nightlife in the Flats along the infamous yet no-longer-flammable Cuyahoga River. Nobody could believe they were actually in Cleveland!

The 2001 Harvard Business School Global Alumni Conference in Cleveland, Ohio, is still considered the best ever. The school has since changed the name of the conference to the Global Leadership Forum, or GLF. I think they did that so no one in the future would be embarrassed if they couldn't live up to Cleveland.

Imagine, Cleveland, once again a place people actually want to live UP to.

-55-

That Was Then, This Is Now

SINCE I'VE BEEN retired for some years now, I have noticed that there is one thing I currently have in abundance: I have the luxury of time. And I seem to spend an awful lot of it reading about and/or watching world events.

Once in a while I get wrapped up in politics, cringe at the latest embarrassing scandal in Washington, DC, or lament the fact that manufacturing has made a mass exodus overseas (a pet peeve, I admit).

When this occurs, I want to dive into the nearest phone booth, don my cape and tights, and *do something*. I want to *act*–until the moment I realize that in order save the world, I actually have to get out of my chair.

(Well, I did recently rejoin the NRA–just in case. I hope I'm not sorry I gave all my guns away.)

I have even caught myself, on more than one occasion, watching Fox News and saying to Shirl, "Hey, I have an idea. What if they . . . ?"

And "What if we . . . ?"

"Hey, what would happen if . . . ?"

Then one night, it hit me.

Shut up and write your book, Don.

APPENDIX

Engineering Society Honor

Advisory Board Tribute

Engineering Society

Honors

Former Lincoln Electric Chief

DONALD F. HASTINGS, well-known as a Cleveland business leader but not as an engineer, has been honored with the Cleveland Engineering Society's 1998 Leadership Award.

It is not unusual for Hastings, Chairman Emeritus of The Lincoln Electric Company, to be recognized far afield as a result of his wide range of interests and activities. When he enters into projects, it is with a surge of enthusiasm that makes itself known and gets things done.

"I'm really excited to receive this honor without being a graduate engineer," Hastings said. He was honored for being a leader in welding technology and for encouraging engineers to develop good products.

Still, there are strong engineering vibes in his background.

He joined Lincoln in 1953 as a trainee in its welding school after getting a master's degree in marketing from Harvard Business School. His MBA followed graduation from California's Pomona College, where he earned a degree in economics.

"I guess I became an engineer by osmosis," he said. "I really enjoyed the technical aspects of the process at Lincoln."

After he got the Lincoln job, he took courses in electrical engineering and welding metallurgy at the University of California at Berkeley.

He won national recognition during the era of massive corporate downsizing and layoffs with his belief that it was the wrong direction.

"Your best way of running a business," he said yesterday, "is making employees as important as the shareholders and the customers. Too many companies are run strictly for the bottom line and what security analysts think. The reason Lincoln has been successful for 102 years is that they put their people on an equal basis with their investors. They are not just tools to be hired and fired at will."

He said he got a charge when Al "Chainsaw" Dunlap, known as the king of corporate job cutting, "got his comeuppance" and was fired as chairman of Sunbeam Corporation this week.

As a businessman keenly aware of changing trends, Hastings plunged vigorously and enthusiastically into the global marketplace.

"America can stay a leading industrial power," he said, "through technological innovation that beats the low manufacturing costs of third world countries."

Don Hastings is Chairman and Chief Executive Officer of the Cleveland Council of World Affairs and is on the executive committee of the Greater Cleveland Growth Association. He has been Chairman of the International Trade Alliance and World Trade Center.

Cleveland Plain Dealer, June 17, 1998

Donald F. Hastings

Chairman and Chief Executive Officer
The Lincoln Electric Company
Advisory Board Honor

T HE EMPLOYEES OF The Lincoln Electric Company appreciate your confidence in our ability to work our way out of the difficult financial situation we faced for the past two years.

When others were negative, you were steadfast in your belief that every department would rise to a new level, knowing full well that we would be severely challenged to meet your expectations as well as customer demand.

We are proud to have lived up to your expectations by achieving record sales and earnings per share in 1994.

This once again proves that *the possible is immense* as we commit to accomplishing even greater results in 1995, our centennial year.

Thank you for leading us to an outstanding performance!

THE ADVISORY BOARD on behalf of the finest employees in the world.

The citation was signed by the president and twenty-seven advisory board representatives of the company.

"Walt Disney was right. It *is* kind of fun to do the impossible!"

~Donald F. Hastings